**CBI SERIES IN MANAGEMENT COMMUNICATIONS**

Mastering the Business and Technical Presentation

**CBI SERIES IN MANAGEMENT COMMUNICATIONS**

*William J. Gallagher, Series Editor*
Arthur D. Little, Inc.

---

# Mastering the Business and Technical Presentation

Leonard F. Meuse, Jr.

**CBI**

**CBI PUBLISHING COMPANY, INC.**
51 Sleeper Street
Boston, Massachusetts 02210

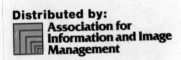

Distributed by:
**Association for
Information and Image
Management**

**Production Editor:** Becky Handler
**Text Designer:** Roy Howard Brown
**Compositor:** Modern Graphics
**Cover Designer:** Betsy Franklin

**Library of Congress Cataloging in Publication Data**

Meuse, Leonard F    1933–
    Mastering the business and technical presentation.

    (CBI series in management communications)
    1. Communication in management.    I. Title.
II. Series.
HF5718.M48        658.4'5        80–18930
ISBN 0–8436–0789–0

Printed in the United States of America

Printing (*last digit*): 9 8 7 6 5 4 3 2

TO DOROTHY

# Contents

# Editor's Foreword

Despite the magnitude and acceleration of change during the past two decades, the functions of management remain essentially the same: to make decisions, to plan, to organize, to get things done, and to measure the results. Before decisions can be made, however, information must be transferred. Before tasks can be accomplished, behavior may have to be modified. And communication is still the only means we have to reach these objectives.

The basic problem with communication stems from how we view the process. The first image the term evokes is usually of someone speaking or writing. Implicit in this image, of course, is that this activity is directed at someone else in the background. But the emphasis is on the transmitter rather than on the receiver. According to this perception, communication is always one-directional.

This perception assumes that to communicate, all we need to do is talk or write. The corollaries of this assumption are that the message intended is always conveyed and that logic and clarity are enough to guarantee persuasion. Consequently, a great deal of the training in oral and written communication has been oriented toward the speaker or writer. Guidelines for the listener or reader are usually ignored.

This text is one of a series based on the premise that no one merely communicates. Rather, he or she communicates something to someone. And that someone—the listener or reader—is very important. He or she is not, as many apparently believe, a passive element receiving information without coloring or response. On the contrary, the receiver is continually reacting to the expression of ideas in light of personal experience, interests, and values. Therefore, in any communication the receiver adds their own dimension to the meaning and then responds to what he or she has added. Communication is thus interactive, and being interactive, it requires the cooperation of sender and receiver.

Effective communication ensures cooperation by anticipation and adaptation. It considers the communication objective, the subject, and the audience. It recognizes the environment in which the communication is to take place, the external and internal factors that affect it, and the extent of the control needed by both sender and receiver to neutralize these factors. It recognizes that selecting the appropriate medium is as important as tailoring the presentation.

This communication series was prepared in recognition of the fact that the receiver is the most important element in communication, for he or she is not only the reason for the communication but the measure by which its success is evaluated. In the texts designed to help the sender, the guidelines are aimed at improving skills by anticipating problems posed by the receiver. In the texts designed for the receiver, the guidelines are aimed at improving the ability to assimilate information by cooperating with the sender.

The authors of the CBI Series in Management Communications have a distinctive combination of skills as practitioners and teachers. Each is employed by an organization that places heavy emphasis on communication. Each has also spent many years in teaching communication through formal academic courses and through seminars sponsored by government and industry. Collectively, they possess diverse experience in industry, government, and education.

The texts therefore address the needs of business and government and the various circumstances in which these needs for communication skills are evident. Each of the authors is aware of these needs not only because of his position, but because of the numerous opportunities he has had to discuss them with others at various levels of management. The guidelines presented, therefore, offer a realistic and practical approach to effective communication.

The texts can be used as guides for self-training or as the basis for formal group training in college classes or in seminars sponsored by government and industry. Although written independently with only broad guidelines and coordination by the editor, they have a unity of purpose and design. The books can therefore be used collectively by those interested in the broad spectrum of communication or individually by those with selected interests.

Since all of the authors are realists, we do not offer guidelines as magic potions guaranteeing instantaneous success. Principles and techniques do not ensure success. Motivation and a great deal of effort are also required. Our objective is to show you the way; the goal is yours to attain.

*William J. Gallagher,* Editor
CBI Series in Management Communications

# Preface

## How to Create a Disaster without Trying Hard at All

Perhaps you feel that turning a presentation into the second maiden voyage of the *Titanic* is easy. You're wrong; it takes dedication, imagination, inspiration. Let me describe just a few of the requirements.

- Don't waste time by considering the *objective* of your presentation. Get down to business immediately.

- Don't engage in futile exercises such as *analyzing your audiences' background and attitudes*. These intellectual games only confuse and immobilize you.

- Don't be burdened with *strategy*. When you deliver your presentation, you will carry the day.

- Never lose precious time in *organizing* your information. No one bothers with outlines anymore. Besides, even if you do make an outline you will ignore it anyway. Plan something today and the situation will change tomorrow, rendering the plan useless.

- By all means, don't prepare a *script*. There isn't time for that. Besides, it's overkill. The important thing is to get some visuals that you can talk to. Some of the visuals are already available from past presentations.

- If you start worrying about *physical factors*—such as rooms, projectors, screens, and seats—you will take valuable time away from your other duties. After all, your job comes first!

- Don't be overly concerned about delivering the presentation. This too is a waste of time. Just get up and speak your piece. You don't have to be an actor to explain accounts receivable or lab experiments. Anybody can speak to a group of people.

- Don't use fancy visuals. They make you look like you're in show business. You will create the wrong impression entirely.

- Never have a dry run. This wastes not just your time, but also that of everyone else involved. Not only that, your practice presentation is likely to be better than the real thing.

- Above all, don't get ready too soon. The longer you wait, the more current your data will be. Any good executive has to be flexible.

If, on the other hand, you number yourself among the people who are not especially fond of disasters, the material in these pages will help you. This book is a field manual on how to communciate with audiences. It is a compilation of tactics, suggestions, ideas, tips, checklists, and biases accumulated over many years of working with speakers and audiences. The book's goal is not to be theoretical—full of high-sounding, profound insights—but to be practical and genuinely useful. It deals with two questions:

1. What is the best way to *prepare* an audiovisual presentation?
2. What are the techniques of *delivering* a business or technical presentation that will ensure success in informing and persuading audiences?

Much of the information in these pages is the product of memorable mistakes as well as gratifying successes. My aim is that you avoid the mistakes and create some successes of your own.

Please dog-ear the pages.

# Acknowledgments

My thanks go to Eileen Menezes, whose keen mind, sharp eye, and talented fingers created a manuscript out of a pile of smudged papers; to David Crocker, whose artwork graces some of these pages; to my wife, Dot, whose patience and support made this book possible; and to the hundreds of speakers and audiences with whom I have worked. These pages are filled with the things we taught each other.

# 1
# The Dynamics of a Presentation

Let's begin with a few definitions of terms that pertain to the presentation. An *audiovisual presentation* is a communications medium in which an audience receives messages through two channels: the eyes and the ears. This book is a practical guide on how to reach audiences through *live* audiovisual presentations. For brevity, the book will use the single word *presentation,* instead of audiovisual presentation. Beyond the mere mechanics of the two channels, a presentation is a deliberate act in which carefully planned sounds and images serve to focus the attention of an audience on a subject for a brief period. It is the designed collaboration of auditory and visual impressions that can give a presentation the power to hold the attention of—and more importantly, to inform and persuade—an audience.

A *speech* is a presentation without a formal visual channel. The audience receives visual information, but at random. The principal visual focus is, of course, the speaker. An effective speaker can provide enough visual interest to hold the attention of an audience, but the lack of a *programmed* visual channel allows the audience to spend much of its time concentrating on trivialities, such as the color of the speaker's tie, the shape of the lighting fixture, or the expressions on the faces of other people.

A *meeting* usually has even less structure (and, often less direction). At meetings, the "presenter" and the "audience" are in constant flux, since each attendee is expected to both listen and contribute. It is important to mention meetings here for two reasons. First, the presentation is often used as a prelude to a meeting. We will deal later with the problem of preventing a presentation from deteriorating into a meeting prematurely. Second, in many meetings, visuals are used to focus attention on a problem or question. The people in attendance work on the problem using the projected image as a visual worksheet. Projectors and screens alone do not a presentation make.

1

To repeat: a presentation consists of a series of deliberately planned sounds and images, and for our purposes, is delivered to an audience live.

## WHY A PRESENTATION?

Do you really need to give a presentation? Other less expensive methods can convey your message. Why not a memo? A report? A series of phone calls? A meeting?

No, somehow these other methods will not do. Written communication is acceptable for lesser tasks, such as monthly reports and requests for paper clips. (Besides, nobody reads anymore.) Phone calls have their place, too; but when the stakes are big enough, face-to-face communication is indispensable. Meetings are useful for achieving group understanding or approval and even for working on a problem. But they lack the focus, direction, and impact that a presentation can provide.

We are slow to acknowledge the power of the presentation. A presentation is often called a "Dog and Pony Show" or a "Show and Tell." (After all, we are in business and not "Show Business.") Yet, the predominant form of structured communication in large companies is the presentation. In fact, if you are a vice president (or above) in a major company, it is likely that much of your job involves attending presentations.

Why are presentations so pervasive in industry? One reason is *feedback*. What little feedback you do get from memos and reports is often days or even weeks in coming. Presentations give you immediate information, and not just on your proposal, plan, idea, or problem. Other kinds of useful reactions, both spoken and unspoken, can include these comments:

"I disagree."

"I don't understand."

"I'm bored."

"It's a good plan if you can convince my boss."

You need two levels of feedback in any communication situation. The first level concerns how well your audience has received and understood your message. The second deals with how that audience reacts to the information. The presentation has the powerful advantage of gathering all the participants in a proposed course of action or all the principals in a decision-making process and:

1. Ensuring uniform understanding
2. Reaching group judgment
3. Obtaining the reaction of a group (e.g., to a problem)
4. Solving a problem (or pointing one out)
5. Obtaining approval or arriving at a decision
6. Gaining acceptance for a program, idea, activity, plan
7. Resolving conflicts
8. Assigning responsibility

What makes a presentation special is that *people* have convened to focus on a subject (and often to interact). The speaker gets immediate feedback, and so do the participants.

Another reason for the widespread use of presentations in business is *impact*. You could write a report, for example, and in the conclusion state that "Resolution of the corrosion problem is paramount to the reduction of customer returns with its current negative effect on margins as well as its long-range threat to sales." In an oral presentation you do not have enough time to create long sentences with big words. You would probably summarize your findings quite differently: "The corrosion problem must be solved as quickly as possible. Customer returns are already cutting into our margins. If we don't fix the problem soon, sales will eventually suffer, too."

The immediacy of a presentation allows you to be more spontaneous, more yourself. The audience responds to *you,* as opposed to your words on a piece of paper. The audience, moreover, can sense what is important to you because the stress points, the pauses, and the changes in animation in speech can convey information beyond the mere words.

Beyond speech dynamics, a large part of the impact of a presentation is visual. An audiovisual presentation is a *two-channel* medium. The audience is absorbing and processing what it sees as well as what it hears. Part of the impact is in the visuals such as slides and charts, which will be discussed in detail later. But *you* are part of the visual channel as well. Your appearance, your posture—in fact, anything you do with your body—becomes visual information and is part of the total *impact* of a presentation.

The third reason for the popularity of oral presentations is *control.*

When you write a memo or report, you surrender it to the reader. What will be its fate? Will it be read carefully? Will it be read at all? What distractions in the reader's environment or preoccupations in the reader's mind will interfere with the communication of your message? In an audiovisual presentation, you have the advantage of a captive audience. True, some people may leave the room mentally, but if you work at preparation and delivery, you can exert a great deal of control over the reception of your message. An audiovisual presentation also is a deliberate act. At its best, it is a carefully planned sequence of sounds and images. It is a programmed focussing on a subject for a brief period. Part of its power derives from the fact that the careful integration of audio and visual messages not only provides interest, it also produces a momentum that can compel the attention of an audience. In short—*control*.

The final advantage of the audiovisual presentation is that it is *easier* than reading. Most people prefer to get information from a presentation—even a canned presentation—than from reading. To "get information" is to learn. Learning is a three-step process:

1. *Recognition*—Receiving and identifying each signal.
2. *Association*—Relating the signals to our total experience. More simply, this step involves "pulling the file" we keep on each signal, reviewing the contents of that file, and relating it to the immediate situation.
3. *Understanding*—A new awareness based on the patterns formed by all the signals in a message.

Why the use of *signal* and not *word*? Because much of what we learn is based not just on words, but on *nonverbal* signals—gestures, facial expressions, vocal intonations, body language. Words on paper cannot possess the richness and variety of nonverbal communication. The reader is thus deprived of both the *information* and the *stimulation* that nonverbal signals provide.

At a basic level of recognition, it is less *physical* work to listen to words than it is to read them. Anyone who has had the experience of fighting to keep the eyelids open and struggling to drive the eyes across the rigid lines, page after page, knows that reading can be hard work. Of course, physical factors can make listening hard, too. A speaker's volume, pace, articulation, and vocal dynamics can affect listenability; so can the acoustics of the room. But, except for extreme problem cases, listening is *physically* easier than the rigid, linear, one-dimensional demands of reading.

Can a person associate signals better when listening as opposed to reading? Have you ever had the experience of "reading" a book and suddenly discovering that you don't have the vaguest notion of what you "read" in the last three paragraphs? Perhaps this is an unfair question. You have also been "listening" to a speaker and experienced similar lapses. Association is hard work no matter how we receive the signals. Association is the mental work we must do to extract meaning from the physical signals that make up communication. Many factors can affect the process, including our energy level, our interest in the subject, the importance of the information to us, the credibility we assign to the source, and the presence or absence of distractions, bias, and/or preoccupation. These factors can frustrate communication for reader and listener alike.

But in an *effective* presentation, the immediacy, the dynamics, the interplay of verbal and nonverbal signals, the power of combining visual and vocal information can help audience members focus on the material. In short, the same factors that give a speaker a measure of control over the communication process also help the audience do its work of recognizing, associating, and understanding.

### Why the Enormous Reliance on the Audiovisual Presentation in Industry and Government?

Because it works. The presentation is a highly efficient method of communication. It permits immediate feedback, helps the speaker to communicate with the impact of two-channel immediacy, allows a measure of control over the communication process, and is easier for the audience to process.

## THE DEATH OF WRITING?

Presentations are *not* the answer to every business communication problem. Writing is not dying; it doesn't even have a cold! Presentations do have some serious disadvantages, three of which will be discussed here.

### Problem One: Presentations Disappear

Since they consist of spoken words and brief images, presentations are impermanent phenomena. Your audience will recall perhaps 30 percent of the material in a presentation after one hour. Within a week, 95 percent will be forgotten. An audience remembers the main theme of a presentation along with the major supporting themes and the significant highlights, never the details. Presentations are useless as reference sources.

One currently fashionable practice is to provide the audience with "hard copies" of the visuals used in the presentation. Certainly, if reference materials are needed this is better than nothing, but as you will discover later, if the visuals are well designed, they will not be useful as reference documents. Conversely, materials that serve as excellent reference sources are usually disastrous as visuals.

If achieving your communication goal requires providing reference material, *write* it. Writing also provides a *record*. The business purpose of a communication often requires the permanency of a written document. Presentations, no matter how influential they may be in affecting the course of an organization, leave no record; they leave a series of impressions.

### Problem Two: Presentations are Expensive and Work Best with Limited Audiences

If your task is to assure that all 50,000 members of your company understand the new Retirement Plan, the sheer logistical problems make a presentation, or even a series of them, highly impractical.

In 1959, the president of a Massachusetts-based corporation gave an audiovisual presentation to the entire company—about 2,000 people—in Symphony Hall, Boston. Today, the company numbers around 15,000 and its members are scattered over the globe. A similar presentation would require half of Fenway Park to accommodate the audience. And, even though the electronic scoreboard could be used for the visuals, the sheer expense of assembling that number of people makes the project unthinkable.

Clearly, the most efficient way to reach very large audiences is through the ancient (and still thriving) device of writing. If the stakes are high enough, however, presentations to three or four thousand people will work. Today's audiovisual technology has made reaching huge audiences possible, but the expense is equally huge, especially if the audience is being paid to attend!

Presentations in general are expensive. The artwork, photography, physical setting, and equipment can be costly, and the *audience* is also an expense. Very often, even a short presentation to a group of corporate officers can cost hundreds of dollars in their salaries alone. Therefore, before deciding to use a presentation, consider the costs and the logistics, then ask how your objectives can be accomplished using another medium, such as a report, brochure, memo, bulletin, booklet, procedure, or manual.

### Problem Three: The Pace is Sender-Controlled

In a presentation, the audience has no control over the pace of delivery. Readers, on the other hand, can move at their own speed and can reread difficult passages. Listeners have no such luxury. If the speaker is talking too rapidly, audiences quickly become fatigued and drop out mentally. If the speaker is talking too slowly, audience members begin to use the extra time to think about other things. They take brief mental excursions and return to the presentation without missing anything important. Eventually, however, they return too late. Some essential information is lost and the problem is compounded by a speaker who is dawdling and droning on. The result is the same as with a too rapid delivery—the audience drops out mentally.

Of course, if a speaker is able to tailor the pace of the delivery to the needs of the audience, problem three no longer is a problem. Based on my observations of hundreds of business presentations, however, improper pace is indeed a problem. In this case, writing may be the answer, especially if the audience is diverse in its background and rates of absorption vary widely. More often, however, the cure is to adopt a pace that will not exhaust the less informed or bore the experts in your audience.

The intent of this chapter is to provide a perspective on audiovisual presentations in contrast with other methods of communication, especially written methods. Table 1 is a quick summary of the main points.

**Table 1** Audiovisual vs. Written Communication

| Advantages | Disadvantages |
|---|---|
| — Immediate Feedback | — Impermanence |
| — Impact | — Impractical for very large audiences |
| — Control over the communication process | — Expensive |
| — Less work for the audience | — Pace is controlled by the speaker |

# HOW FORMAL SHOULD YOUR PRESENTATION BE?

Imagine a spectrum that ranges from the most informal presentation possible to the most rigorously formal. Here is an example of the informal end of the spectrum: A manager convenes subordinates (let's say five supervisors) to review the past week's production figures and to explain the use of a newly modified production control form.

As an example of the opposite end of the spectrum—the most formal presentation—try this: A vice-president must conduct a presentation for the Board of Directors that must justify a new venture for the corporation. The new venture is a controversial, radical departure including a complex technology, new marketing strategies, and a business plan that will require expenditures of $75 million. The new venture has the potential for reversing the company's ominously declining sales and profits.

To be successful, the two presentations should be quite different. And since presentations can fail because they are overly formal or too informal, it is useful to understand the reasons and requirements for giving more or less formal presentations.

## Reasons for a More Formal Presentation

The first—and perhaps the most important—reason that compels a more formal presentation is *the stakes*. The more one may gain or lose, the more formal the presentation is likely to be. Gains or losses can include not only the acceptance or rejection of your proposal, plan, thesis, or idea but also other factors such as the gain or loss of budget allocations, space, capital programs, even personal status. The list, of course, is endless.

The next factor is *audience opposition*. If the task of a presentation is to persuade an audience that is largely predisposed against the presenter's objectives, the need for a more formal approach increases with the strength of that antipathy.

The same is true of factor three, *complexity*. The more an audience must grapple with difficult material, the more one must use the elements of formal presentations.

Factors four and five are related; *audience size* and the need for *repeat performances*. Other factors being equal, the larger the audience, the more formal the presentation. Usually the need for repeat performances also means reaching a larger audience, the difference being that the total audience is addressed sequentially—one audience at a time. In both cases, it is usually important to ensure that a large group of people reaches uniform understanding or agreement on a subject.

Now you can be more analytical in your view of the two examples of informal and highly formal presentations mentioned earlier (see Table 2).

### Requirements for a More Formal Presentation

*A direct relationship exists between the degree of formality of a presentation and the amount of preparation required to produce it.* The

**Table 2** Comparing Degrees of Formality

|  | Informal | Formal |
|---|---|---|
| 1. Stakes | Weekly review plus introduce change in production control form | Extremely high — major venture — company's future at stake — $75 million program |
| 2. Audience opposition | None likely | Yes, it's a "controversial, radical, departure" — requiring "new marketing strategies" |
| 3. Complexity | No problem | A "new, complex technology" must be dealt with, plus a business plan explained |
| 4. Audience size | Five subordinates | The Board of Directors — presumably not large — but enormously influential |
| 5. Repeat Performances? | No | Probably yes . . . if the plan is accepted, others in the organization will require the information.  In fact, the liklihood is that this presentation would be given several times prior to the "final" presentation to the Board of Directors. |

more formal the presentation, the more effort must be devoted to *preparation*. Preparation means:

- Determining the objective of the presentation.
- Analyzing the audience to determine its knowledge level and, if relevant, its attitudes.
- Developing a strategy.
- Organizing the information to achieve the most effective results.
- Preparing a script that integrates the visual and the auditory messages for maximum impact and selecting a visual medium that is appropriate and most effective—for *this* audience, *this* information, *this* objective.
- Carefully considering all of the physical factors that can enhance or frustrate the communication process.
- Conducting a dry run to test the expository and persuasive strengths of the presentation as well as the effectiveness of the delivery.

Every presentation requires some degree of preparation. Even the most informal presentation involves decisions on most of these steps. Sadly, those decisions too often are made randomly and without examination. For example, every presentation has some kind of organization. The mere fact that information must be presented sequentially means that the presenter must *decide* on a sequence. It is quite another matter, however, to begin with the realization that organization is crucial to an audience's understanding and acceptance of one's material, and then to use that realization to decide what information to include, what major and minor headings to use, and what sequences to follow. A presentation, remember, is a *deliberate* act. The elements of preparation are a vital part of that act.

The more formal the presentation becomes, the more emphasis must be placed on effective *delivery,* for audiences tend to view material as an extension of the presenter.

The remainder of this book will deal with these two subjects: techniques for effective *preparation* and techniques for effective *delivery*. The six sequential steps in preparing a presentation are:

1. Define your objective
2. Analyze your audience
3. Consider your tactics

4. Organize your information
5. Prepare the script
6. Consider the physical factors

We will explore each step in the sequence of preparation before turning to the seventh and final step, delivering the presentation to an audience.

# 2
# Step One: Define Your Objective

In the early 1960s, the expression *terminal behavior* came into vogue. The term was used to describe how people performed after taking programmed instruction (self-teaching) courses. Terminal behavior was measured by examinations given to a random cross-section of the people who took the programmed instruction courses, and it was expressed statistically. The idea was to measure human behavior in a limited sphere—in this case, the learning of a body of information. The notion of measuring the results of human communication has fascinated me ever since.

Every presentation results in some form of terminal behavior by each member of the audience. In many cases, the behavior is obvious. In presentations with immediate objectives, such as the allocation of resources, the adoption of a new program, or the response to a problem, the reaction of audience members is usually apparent. They either agree, disagree, or fall somewhere between. This audience reaction is typical of the *persuasive* presentation, in which audience members are asked to decide something and act on that decision in a reasonably predictable way.

Many presentations, however, do not have such immediate and explicit goals. Some presentations seem to be purely *expository,* their only purpose being to convey information to an audience. But even these informational presentations will eventually condition the behavior of audience members in some way; the only questions are "How?" and "How far in the future?" A presentation given to describe the function and activities of your organization, for example, may be wholly informational in content, but the long-range goal may be to foster a greater appreciation of those activities in order to influence decisions that lie far in the future.

12

# WHY ALL THIS TALK OF BEHAVIOR?

Knowing that every presentation should exist in order to influence the behavior of audience members is one key to effective oral communication. In short, the beginning step in an oral presentation should be an inquiry into its ultimate results.

What is the *objective* of your presentation? What do you wish the audience to be aware of, to believe, to *do?* What terminal behavior do you seek? The answers to these questions affect nearly everything you do in preparing for and delivering the presentation. The *objective* becomes the touchstone for all the elements of preparation and the reason for making the presentation. (In fact, the inability to state an objective is an excellent reason for *not* having a presentation.) In other words, once you state your goal in terms of specific audience behavior, everything you do thereafter should focus on achieving that goal. For example, in organizing information, one must make decisions on what information to include. Usually the answers are obvious. Sometimes, however, the information is marginal. In these cases, the question, "Do I need this information to accomplish the objective?" can resolve the indecision. Again, if one uses the ending of the presentation as a final bid to achieve the objective, the ending is more likely to have focus and impact than would otherwise be the case.

The whole inquiry into strategy arises out of the knowledge that the presentation is only one element in a larger complex of communications and human interactions, and that achieving the *objective* often requires more than the mere staging of a slide show. Preparing and delivering an outstanding presentation is never the objective itself; rather, it is a crucial tactic in achieving the objective. Neither is the objective to entertain or amuse, although these tactics, when used with discrimination, may enhance the probability of success in certain situations. The objective lies outside the realm of the presentation itself; it is "audience-centered," not "presenter-centered."

Determining the objective of the presentation is useful in several other ways. Such a process can:

- Help to define the problem, the issue, the need that gives rise to the presentation
- Narrow the scope of the presentation to just the topics necessary to accomplish the goals
- Help to develop a central theme, the first step in organizing the information

- Provide a means of judging and ranking material
- Decide on the appropriate degree of formality
- Provide a standard of success

Determining the objective is important because it is often easy to lose sight of your goal. When the presentation is over, what matters is not how artful the visuals were or how compelling was your delivery; the only criterion of success is the accomplishment of the objective.

## THE OBJECTIVE MUST BE REALISTIC

Example: You are the vice-president of Personnel and are preparing a presentation dealing with the advantages and disadvantages of the four-day workweek for your company. You are convinced that adoption of the four-day workweek is in the best overall interests of the firm, but realize that the idea will be greeted with much skepticism and resistance on the part of top management. What should be the objective of your presentation to a committee of top executives?

If you decide that your objective will be to seek a consensus to establish the four-day workweek immediately, your presentation faces almost certain failure. A more realistic objective might be to obtain agreement to organize a steering committee that would set the guidelines for a pilot experiment with one department. After evaluating the results of this first phase, the decision on whether or not to broaden the scope of the program could be made. In the second case, the presentation is far more likely to meet with success. What is more important, by setting achievable intermediate goals, the ultimate objective becomes attainable.

Objectives are what presentations are about.

# 3
# Step Two: Analyze Your Audience

Once the objective has been determined, the focus logically turns to the audience because the *audience* must accomplish the objective. If it were within your power to achieve your goal alone, you would not be spending your time preparing a presentation!

To be successful, any communication must be audience-centered, whether it be a formal presentation or a notice on the bulletin board. Knowing what sort of terminal behavior you seek from an audience is a beginning. You must also know how to reach that particular audience. Step two, therefore, deals with building profiles of and communicating with various audiences.

Presentations appeal to both the intellect and the emotions. True, the themes of most business presentations are based on logical premises, but emotional factors are almost always present. Constructing an audience profile, therefore, is an attempt to determine the knowledge and the attitudes of audience members.

## AUDIENCE BACKGROUND

What does your audience know about your subject? You can think about audience background in two ways:

1. What is the *general* level of understanding of your topic?
2. What do typical audience members know about your *specific* plan, proposal, design, thesis, program, idea?

The answers to these questions are important because they dictate one key to reaching an audience: *level of detail*.

How much detail must you provide to ensure that your audience can follow your exposition? This is not an easy question to answer even under the most obvious circumstances. For example, while reading the newspaper one Sunday morning, I strayed from my usual preoccupa- 15 tion with editorial and sports pages and stumbled onto the following set of instructions on how to produce a chemical reaction:

---

### Flan, New Style

| | |
|---|---|
| ½ cup sugar | 1 tall can evap. milk |
| 2 eggs | 1 can cond. milk |
| 1 egg yolk | 1 tsp. vanilla extract |

Put sugar in heavy saucepan and heat, stirring until melted to golden syrup. Put in 1 qt. casserole, beat eggs and yolk together, add evap. milk and with rotary beater, beat mixture into cond. milk. Add vanilla and pour into casserole. Set into pan of hot water and bake in preheated 325° oven 1 hour, or until set. Unmold in serving dish and serve warm (not hot). Serves 6.

---

It was hard to find a place to begin. (My greatest culinary achievement is my internationally famous recipe for toast.) I had considerable difficulty with "one egg yolk," not having the remotest idea of how to get the yellow part free from the white stuff. The fact that the recipe later calls for mixing *all* the eggs is still a source of wonderment.

Here is a partial list of the things that perplexed me that Sunday morning:

Flan, new style (Is there an old style?)

Cond. milk (Does not compute.)

Heavy saucepan (What is a saucepan?)

Casserole (Isn't that something with tuna and noodles?)

Rotary beater (Is there any other kind?)

Until set (Set for what?)

Unmold (I give up.)

What you are witnessing is an *audience* problem. The instructions do not provide a sufficient *level of detail* for me to follow them. Of course, the fault lies not with the author in this case. After all, I had no business peeping about in the cooking section. The shorthand descriptions were completely adequate for the intended audience. If the author had known that a culinary cretin was among the readers, the instructions might well have provided a much greater level of detail: "Separate the yolk from the egg white by cracking the shell into two halves, then slowly pouring the egg white into one of the halves . . ." and so on. Of course, the entire recipe would have required at least twice the space, and what is worse, the usual readers would have been bored by an excessive level of detail.

Technical presentations often pose more problems of audience analysis than do strictly business presentations. Occasionally, some audience members have little general knowledge of the technology and no awareness of the specific application, design, or concept being discussed. The same audience can contain people with advanced knowledge of your subject. The challenge in these cases is to provide a level of detail that will not lose the former or test the patience of the latter too severely. In practice, audiences with huge discrepancies in background are rare; but when such disparities exist, you must cope with them. Here are several suggestions for coping:

- If you must err, always let it be on the side of overcommunication, never the opposite.

- It is best to tailor the level of detail to the least knowledgeable member of the audience *whose understanding is essential to the accomplishment of your objective.*

- It is better to provide more background and supporting detail than less. The well-informed members of your audience are likely to be patient (and even feel magnanimous) if you explain the need for supporting detail at the outset. The opposite course will exclude some members of your audience from participation. Those people whom you exclude will usually become bored and preoccupied or frustrated and angry, depending on their involvement in your subject and their motivation for attending.

- If you face a gulf in understanding so wide that you literally have two audiences, consider giving *two* presentations. The first can be a basic exposition for people needing the special background; the second can then be given to both audiences. Another tactic is to give two presentations in which audience members are chosen by their familiarity with the subject. Of course, the level of detail is tailored in each case to the audience selected.

Even though such formidably disparate audiences are rare, the task of reaching even a normal audience is seldom easy and should never be taken for granted.

You can communicate with other people only on the basis of what you share with them. Indeed, the word *communication* comes from the Latin root *communes,* "to share or to make common." Thus, the success of any communication is directly related to your ability to use what you possess in common with your audience. In practical terms, this means considering what your audience does and does not know about your subject, and occasionally taking steps to find out through informal inquiries or formal surveys. Beyond that, communication means avoiding words likely to be unfamiliar to audience members as well as defining unfamiliar terms whose use is necessary. It means carefully choosing a level of detail that will allow all audience members to participate fully. In the last analysis, communication means the ability to think like—indeed, the ability to become—your audience.

## AUDIENCE DISPOSITION

Not all of your audience problems are related to what the audience knows. Often the obstacles to the terminal behavior you seek lie in the attitudes of audience members. In fact, the more persuasive the presentation becomes (as opposed to expository or information-giving), the more critical becomes the analysis of audience attitudes.

How does your audience *feel* about your idea, proposal, plan, scheme, conclusion, notion, theory, solution? Audiences respond to presentations both intellectually and emotionally. We appeal to their sense of logic on the one hand to convince them of the correctness of our arguments. We also appeal to their sense of pride, fear, isolation, indignation, compassion, gregariousness, and a host of other emotions to convince them of the persuasiveness of our arguments.

How much persuading must you do? The answer lies in the attitudes of the people who come into the room to experience your presentation. Specifically, what are their attitudes (preconceptions, biases, prejudices) toward your *objective* and—often as important— what are their attitudes toward *you?* The more antipathy you face toward your proposal, the more work you must do to win over the audience. Where one example might suffice, three may now be needed. If you face a personal credibility problem with an audience, you must call on the testimony of other people when available and work constantly to establish your own stature as an expert in your subject.

It almost never happens, but the worst possible audience you can face is one in which the four elements of your analysis all yield problems:

1. The audience possesses very little general understanding of your subject.
2. They have no technical knowledge of your specific proposal.
3. Your audience is opposed generally to your proposal.
4. Most of them are convinced that you possess the brains of a radish!

## SUMMARY

Either by instinct or by design, every good communicator develops the ability to construct a mental image of a typical audience member and then uses that image to test every word, every sentence, every idea. In presentations, the craft of audience centeredness goes beyond considerations of audience background and attitudes. It pervades the entire process: organization, script preparation, physical factors, delivery, and even handling questions. In the long run, the more audience-centered you become, the more successful you are likely to be.

In summary, the keys to reaching an audience are three:

1. Know your audience's background.
2. Know your audience's disposition.
3. Become your audience. Talk their language. Use the proper level of detail and weight of evidence to inform and persuade them.

# 4
# Step Three: Consider Your Tactics

A presentation is an intense concentration on a subject for a brief period, a deliberate act involving the programming of an audio as well as a visual channel. But in a larger sense, a successful presentation extends beyond the walls of the room in which it takes place and beyond the brief time in which the sounds and images occur. Why? Because a presentation involves the behavior of the participants.

It is short-sighted to expect that the presentation alone will accomplish your objective. At this stage, you must ask: What options are available to me and what actions can I take *beyond the act of the presentation itself* to help accomplish my objective? These actions are collectively called the *tactics of a presentation.* We will touch on several kinds of tactics, but the choice of actions is endless. What is essential is the realization that the choices and the actions are available. You must choose and you must act. Otherwise, the realm of tactics is abandoned to the vagaries of chance.

## HOW MANY PRESENTATIONS?
Let us begin our examination of tactical options with a simple question: Are you more likely to accomplish your objective with a single presentation, or with a series of them, each one building toward the final adoption, acceptance, and approval of your proposal?

Example: Several years ago, it became my task to propose a system of technical information for a new plant with a highly sophisticated technical product. The plant manager had three principal subordinates, each with major operational responsibilities. We could easily have formulated a final plan for the plant and presented it to the four senior people in one heart-stopping roll of the dice. Instead, we chose to present our proposal to one of the three principal subordinates. After receiving his comments and suggestions and incorporating them in the proposal, we repeated the presentation and the feedback process for the second, then the third member of the plant manager's staff. At last, we were ready for "The Presentation" before the plant manager and the three senior managers. The final version was a ritual of review and confirmation on the part of the audience.

Part of your tactical analysis should be to decide how many presentations are necessary, and to whom.

## TIMING

When should you conduct the presentation? Often, the timing of a presentation is beyond your control. Usually you do not have sufficient time to prepare completely. To the extent you can control the time of the presentation, you should do so with these two thoughts in mind:

- Always allow yourself enough time to prepare properly; the results of hasty and incomplete preparation are always apparent in the end product.

- Time the presentation for the maximum impact. Avoid times when other events might cause key members of your audience to be absent.

## WHO SHOULD ATTEND?

If the presentation is informational, who needs the information? If the objective is to work on a problem, what human resources will you need to understand its complexities and put forth the effort to solve it?

On rare occasions, you may wish to exclude someone from the presentation. It is conceivable that someone can be so intractably opposed to your objective that his or her presence will frustrate it. Another example is the individual who constantly dominates a problem-solving session to the extent that nearly everyone else's ideas are stifled. It may not always be possible to exclude such problem people from your audience; but when it is, do it! You may choose to send a secondary group of people a summary of the presentation, even including copies of your visuals; your "problem person," of course, would be so informed.

In practice, however, it is seldom that easy, because accomplishing your objective usually requires the support and cooperation of such people. In any event, you can never exclude anyone whose participation is necessary to accomplishing your objective. Fortunately, there are other alternatives.

## PRELIMINARY INTERVIEWS

Audience members usually fall into one or more of the following classes:

- *Positional*—This person is attending principally because of the position he or she holds in the organization. Often the approval of such a person is crucial to achieving the objective.

- *Representational*—This audience member attends to represent a part of the organization and hence the point of view of that group (department, division). The representational member is charged with protecting the interests of the group.

- *Sacrificial*—Occasionally your audience will include one or more members who will have to give up something, such as control, desirable space, position, a cherished program, staff or operating funds, if your objective is achieved. Clearly, this kind of audience member is one of the most difficult to persuade or motivate.

- *Responsible*—This audience member will be asked to do something, such as carry out a program, achieve a goal, assume more responsibility, or conduct a study. This person's reaction to the presentation will be directly linked to how the new responsibility will be perceived. A challenging and rewarding project is likely to be viewed much more favorably than an increase in workload without additional resources.

Most business presentations deal with either bringing about or coping with change. When you are planning such a presentation, consider these questions: Who will be asked to change? Who will be asked to sacrifice or to assume more responsibility or simply to take on more work? Whose support will you need? Who will be opposed to your objective?

These and similar questions point to the importance of meeting with such pivotal people *before* the presentation. Preliminary meetings with individuals or small groups can help you discover the sources of support or opposition to your objective. They can also help you learn or confirm the roles that key audience members will play. The ideal tactic is to exchange information and seek either participation or acceptance. Very often, thirty minutes over coffee cups can ensure the success of months of work.

Bear in mind that resolving the inevitable problems of change is best begun at the individual level in preference to the group level. The inhibitions of individuals in group processes as well as the momentum that can occur in groups make it difficult to deal with the deep-seated resistance, biases, or objections of individual members. Again, the value of meeting with pivotal members of your audience before the presentation should always be considered when difficulties lay in the path of accomplishing your objective.

## OVERCOMING OBSTACLES TO ACHIEVING YOUR GOAL

### Adversaries

My belief has always been that people who are *open* in their opposition to your plan, proposal, idea are to be numbered among your friends. Spending time with such "adversaries" will help uncover flaws in your arguments, weaknesses in your case, chinks in your armor. By all means work with such adversaries, not just to convert them, but also to use their thinking to modify and sharpen your presentation.

### Negative Information

Tactically, one of the worst decisions you can make is to omit negative information. If you include only the information *supporting* your objective, you will most surely lose credibility with members of your audience, especially if their questions open up whole areas of inquiry that you have chosen to ignore in the presentation. To suceed, your presentation must be objective.

But how does one deal with negative information? To begin, it is important to view your presentation as a lawyer does a case. What are the most telling arguments? What are the pivotal issues? What are the weaknesses in the case? What questions can be expected from the audience? What hurdles must be cleared to achieve the objective?

Next, for tactical purposes, divide the negative information into two categories:

1. Points that are potentially damaging to your case
2. Secondary concerns, questions, and objections

Information in the first category *must* be included in the presentation. Not doing so will result in an obviously one-sided presentation and a loss of credibility. The proper tactic is to demonstrate that the negative information has been carefully considered and, when weighed against all other factors, it does not alter your conclusions or recommendations.

Information in the second category need not be included in the presentation; but if it is not, be prepared to answer questions comprehensively and convincingly. Once again, be ready to show that the point has been considered and, for whatever reason, rejected or defused.

## SUMMARY

It is impossible to imagine every situation in which tactics serve as the vital element in achieving your objective. But one fact is certain: it is naive to assume that the presentation alone will carry the day. Part of a comprehensive preparation should always involve being aware of and exploring *all* the opportunities that exist in order to overcome obstacles and to ensure success.

# 5
# Step Four: Organize Your Information

## WHY BOTHER?

For a variety of reasons, most people do not like to spend time organizing presentations:

- "The press of time doesn't permit it."
- "It's too much trouble."
- "The return isn't worth the effort."
- "I know what I want to say; it's all organized in my head."
- "It won't make that much difference."

The curious fact, however, is that *every* presentation has some kind of organization—intentional or not—because every presentation requires three elements:

1. *Material Selection*—The choice from a large body of available information of only those facts, arguments, and details deemed necessary to achieve the objective.
2. *Topics*—The choice of major and minor subject headings under which all the information is discussed.
3. *Sequence*—The choice of an order in which to convey the information.

Notice that each element requires making choices. Since every presentation involves material selection, topics, and sequence, every presentation is the product of such choices. The only question is, will you make these choices consciously and carefully, or will you decide to "wing it"? Your best course is to consider your choices and to make them deliberately. The alternative is . . . Well, let me demonstrate.

25

## THE ZOOMIE PACKAGING COMPANY

Imagine that your chief manufacturing engineer has the task of evaluating a new packaging machine for your company. After an investigation, the findings and recommendations are to be presented to the manufacturing management committee, perhaps in the following way.

---

Good morning, ladies and gentlemen. My trip to the Zoomie Packaging Machinery Company was most enlightening. I arrived at Trenton at about 3:48 P.M. last Tuesday, the twelfth. Mr. Zoomie was most helpful and informative. His chief engineer, Fred Feeble, met me at the airport. He seemed most capable technically. Fred recommended the Globe Hotel—an excellent choice, although their food didn't measure up to their service.

Next morning—the thirteenth—I saw the new model Z-2300, Automatic, In-Line Packaging System. This is an excellent state-of-the-art design. The use of digital logic controls plus high-speed overwrapping make the Z-2300 the most advanced packaging machine in the industry. Fred explained that it took three years and 12 million dollars to develop it.

The Zoomie people were most gracious and accommodating, answering all of my questions completely. I was most impressed by Fred Feeble and his design team, who felt they were able to adapt the Z-2300 to our specific packaging application.

Conservative estimates indicate that the Zoomie Z-2300 will increase packaging capacity by 18 percent. That evening in my hotel room, I calculated that our present five machines can be replaced by four Zoomies with a labor reduction of 20 percent.

I am convinced that the reliability record of the Zoomie Z-2300 will exceed that of our present machines. Fred Feeble assured me that four machines can be delivered and installed at our facility within 180 days. Zoomie's record of support and customer service is the envy of the industry.

Of course, the fact that the Zoomie Z-2300 is a high-speed, positive-action packaging system means that about 35 percent of our ice cream cones will be crushed in packaging. Unfortunately, the system is inappropriate for our application, even though the Zoomie technology is most impressive.

We can hope that eventually the Zoomie people will develop a packaging machine for fragile goods such as our number one sugar cones. The graciousness and cooperation of the people at Zoomie impressed me greatly. They are an excellent firm to do business with. My return flight on the morning of the fourteenth was uneventful.

---

## WHAT IS THE PROBLEM?

What seems to be at fault with this presentation? The obvious answer is, "It is poorly organized." But that is too easy. The deeper problem—in fact, the most common problem with defective organization—is that it is self-centered and not *audience-centered*.

If you review the Zoomie presentation, your first impression might be one of aimless rambling. The impression is not quite correct. The presentation does have a loose organization. It is a rough chronology of the trip to Trenton. Woven into the trip story with all its irrelevancies are bits of analysis of the Z-2300. The elements are all given from the *presenter's point of view*. From the audience's viewpoint, the most important information comes near the end of the presentation and even then, almost as an afterthought.

Effective organization always begins with this question: "What does my audience need?" In the Zoomie case, the answer comes in three parts:

1. Do you recommend that we substitute the Zoomie Z-2300 for our present packaging machine? and
2. Why? (or why not?)
3. What additional details are worth knowing?

In our make-believe case, these three classes of information look like this:

1. *Must know*—I do not recommend that we substitute the Zoomie Z-2300 for our present packaging machines.
2. *Important to Know*—The Z-2300 is a high-speed, positive-action packaging system that will crush about 35 percent of our ice cream cones.
3. *Nice to Know*—(details that were not provided in the original presentation):

Does Zoomie have another model that can meet our needs?

Can Zoomie modify one of their packaging systems to handle our sugar cones?

Is Zoomie willing to develop a high-speed ice cream cone packaging system? If so, roughly how much would it cost and how long would it take?

Are any other packaging systems manufacturers being considered? Who?

It is useful to think of the three classes of information as a target (see Figure 1).

A well-organized presentation is *audience-centered*. It begins with the bullseye and works outward. Thus, the audience gets the most needed information immediately, followed by supporting facts or arguments. Highlights and significant details come last. Information outside the third ring does not belong in the presentation (the food and service at the Globe Hotel notwithstanding).

Organization is the craft of selecting and arraying information and arguments in a way that satisfies the needs of your audience.

## THE BEGINNING

The cliche about the persistence of first impressions surely applies to presentations. A feeble or confusing beginning usually creates a lasting impression, one that may be impossible to overcome. How, then, should you begin?

Once again, begin with the needs of your audience. Here is a list of

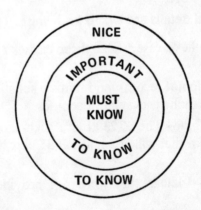

**Figure 1** Three Classes of Information

what every audience has a right to know in the first minute of a presentation.

*Who Are You?*—If the audience does not know you, introduce yourself. It may also be necessary to provide a *brief* note about yourself to help establish credibility in your subject area. Do so only when you deem it necessary. Of course, if the audience does know you, don't waste their time with introductions.

*What Are You Up To?*—What is the subject of your presentation? What is its *purpose?* What are you trying to accomplish? What is the problem, if any? From the audience's viewpoint, answer the question, "Why should I sit through this presentation?"

*What Is the Scope of the Presentation?*—What subject territory will be covered? Remember, not every aspect of a subject will always be covered. For example, a presentation might cover the cost/benefit analysis of a capital investment but, because of insufficient data, not deal with the environmental questions. In such a case, the scope statement should point out what the presentation *will not* cover. Not to do so is to invite unnecessary and embarrassing questions, interruptions, and digressions.

*What are the Criteria?*—In some presentations, the objective requires that the audience accept conclusions and support recommendations based on the analysis and arguments you present. In this kind of presentation, the audience must know the rules of the game before it begins. The criteria are the judgments on which the issue will be decided, such as cost, efficiency, morale, effect on product quality, technical feasibility, and/or profitability; the list is endless. The criteria, or decisive factors, for your specific presentation should be cited in the first minute.

*What Do You Expect of Me?*—Every audience member deserves to know what his or her role will be. Put yourself in the shoes of your audience. Am I expected to merely absorb information for my own use, or will I be expected to use it to help solve a problem? Will I be expected to make a decision? Commit resources? Comment on the feasibility of a proposal or design? Knowing one's role at the outset of a presentation helps an audience member relate to the material properly. Moreover, the terminal behavior you expect at the conclusion becomes immediately apparent.

People tend to remember what they experience at the beginnings and the ends of things. The lesson is simple: Do not waste beginnings and endings; use them to accomplish your objective.

## THE MIDDLE

With the preliminaries out of the way, the middle, or body, of the presentation can now assume its role of informing and/or persuading the audience. Think of a presentation as a sandwich: the beginning and end come from a bakery; the *kind* of sandwich you eat is determined by what goes in the middle.

As mentioned at the start of this chapter, organizing information calls for three kinds of decisions or choices:

Material selection: What information goes into a presentation?

Topics: What are the major and minor headings?

Sequence: What is the order in which the information will be presented?

The end product of all this choosing is an *outline,* which will serve as your roadmap when you prepare the script for your presentation. Several methods can help you create that roadmap. Several patterns of organization will be suggested later in this chapter. For the moment, however, let's concentrate on the simple idea of *themes.*

Every presentation has a *main theme.* The main theme is the nucleus, the central idea, or assertion on which the entire presentation is built. Often, the best way to begin the middle of a presentation is to state its main theme:

We should install dust-control equipment in the production area.

This technique is helpful not only because it distills out the essence of the presentation, but also because it provides a statement of your objective (in this case, to obtain approval to spend $400,000 for dust-control equipment).

The next question is "Why?" "We should install dust control equipment in the production area because:"

1. It will reduce quality control production losses by 22 percent (net annual savings: $275,000).
2. It will reduce customer returns by nearly 10 percent (net annual savings: $35,000).
3. It will create a more healthful environment for production workers.

4. Installation of the equipment will not disrupt production.

5. Improved quality will have a beneficial effect on sales.

By placing yourself in the shoes of your audience and asking "why?", you can evolve the supporting, or *subthemes*. Each subtheme (1 through 5) can in turn be organized by asking the question, "Can you prove it?", and then by listing the points necessary to convince your audience of the validity of each subtheme.

The following section provides a more extended example of the use of main theme and subthemes to organize information for a presentation.

## G&T COMPANY, FAIRLAWN PARK

You are the community affairs manager for Goode & True Company, a highly successful manufacturer of scientific instruments. At the moment, your assignment is to help G&T acquire a 60-acre parcel of land in the neighboring Oaktown's Fairlawn Park.

---

Fairlawn Park has long been one of Oaktown's most conspicuous assets. The 300-acre park is studded with lovely old trees and small ponds. However, Oaktown, because of its pressing need to broaden its tax base, has voted to sell a little-used corner of the park to a suitable occupant for seven million dollars.

G&T Company is one of several organizations interested in this highly desirable site. Among the competitors are a rubber company, a highrise apartment developer, a heavy machinery manufacturer, a shopping center developer, and an agent representing about a dozen small businesses, such as distributors, garages, and plastic novelty manufacturers.

Because G&T is such a successful business, the company needs land for expansion of its instrument manufacturing facilities in the immediate future. The Fairlawn Park site is nearly ideal for this purpose in every respect. Accordingly, G&T has hired famous architect, Frank Lloyd Rong, to develop an excellent architectural plan for the site, including attractive buildings that preserve and take advantage of the site's natural beauty. The site development plan also gives careful attention to local traffic patterns. An architectural model as well as several architect's renderings of the buildings are available.

Goode & True has 5,700 employees. An unusually high percentage are professional people, and most of the remainder are involved in the manufacture of complex scientific instruments. Over the twenty-five years since its beginnings as a highly creative company, G&T has established an excellent reputation, not only as a thriving and resourceful business, but also as a forward-looking organization. G&T employees have traditionally become involved in the community affairs of nearby Elmwood, where G&T has its present offices and plant (a complex of very attractive buildings). The company has always been active in Elmwood civic affairs and has made many contributions to worthy local causes.

G&T has an outstanding management team whose efforts over the years have been realized in continuous growth of Sales and Earnings and one of the strongest financial positions in industry.

Virtually all of G&T's manufacturing operations can be labelled light industry. No significant amount of waste materials, pollutants, noise, or odors are produced. The company is quite conscious of its public appearance and has an outstanding record of campus-type site development as well as maintenance and improvement of its properties.

Personnel and pay policies are equal to or exceed those of the leading firms in the Oaktown/Elmwood area. G&T employees are not unionized and are quite loyal to the company. Employee turnover is exceptionally low. G&T expects to be adding about 500 people to its payroll over the next three years.

In addition to meeting the seven million dollar purchase price, G&T Company is prepared to spend twelve to fifteen million dollars developing the Fairlawn Park site over a ten-year period, as its world-wide operations expand.

Oaktown is a community of 35,000 residents with many small and even marginal businesses, but not many major industries. Currently, the town is straining to meet the needs for education and municipal services from its hard-pressed tax base.

Apart from some road construction and street lighting, G&T company does not expect to cause a heavy demand for local services. Such things as waste disposal and snow plowing are paid for by the company. No significant increase on the school population is anticipated, and the overall impact on the town's economy appears excellent.

Oaktown's seven selectmen, who range in age from forty-three to sixty-eight years, are, of course, aware of the town's economic problems. All are long-time Oaktown residents; all have the best interests of the town in mind. Three of the seven are owners of small Oaktown businesses; the remaining four are professional men and women.

---

Your task is to convince Oaktown's Board of Selectmen that G&T is the best candidate for the Fairlawn site, for it is the Board of Selectmen who will recommend an occupant to the town in their upcoming report. Their recommendation is expected to be adopted at the next town meeting.

## Organizing the G&T Presentation

Notice that the information in the G&T story is random—without focus, direction, or purpose—as is the case in real situations.

### Step One: A Main Theme

Goode & True Company is a highly desirable choice for the Fairlawn Park site, both as a company and as the developer and occupant of the site.

### Step Two: A Basic Topic Outline

This topic outline is typical of how a first draft might appear.

I. Introduction
II. G&T Company (general)
   A. As an enterprise (what kind of company)
   B. As an organization (what kind of people to do business with)
   C. As a neighbor and community member
   D. As a developer and owner of property
III. G&T as occupant of Fairlawn (specific)
   A. Details of the development plan
   B. Impact on the immediate environment
   C. Impact of G&T on the economy of Oaktown
IV. Summary/Discussion

### *Step Three: An Expanded Outline*

The final task is to expand the subthemes of the topic outline into an *expanded outline* that will serve as the roadmap for preparing the script. Notice that the expanded outline contains some information that was not given originally. This is a delightful by-product of the process of organizing information to achieve an objective.

I. G&T as an enterprise
  A. Brief chronology: emphasis on G&T dynamism, resourcefulness, inventiveness, products, reputation, position in the industry, growth.
  B. Financial strength.
    1. Increase in sales and profits have been consistent over the years.
    2. G&T's assets and net worth: continuous growth.
    3. Current operating and financial statements provide information on the magnitude of G&T operations and profitability.
    4. Future prospects are for continued growth and prosperity.
  C. Current situation: threshold on new expansion.
    1. G&T's expansion plans.
    2. Suitability of Oaktown and Fairlawn Park.

II. G&T as an organization
  A. Corporate philosophy: forward-looking, human dignity, individuality, progressive attitude, minority groups, quality of management, reputation.
  B. Employee relations are excellent.
    1. Pay and benefits: among leaders in industry.
    2. Low employee turnover; a "good place to work."
    3. Employees have a voice; do not feel the need for union representation.
    4. G&T growth due largely to creativity, perseverance, and loyalty of its employees.
  C. Types of employees: professionals, specialists, highly skilled production workers.
  D. G&T has an excellent reputation as an employer.

III. G&T as a neighbor and community member

    A. Relations with other communities have been outstanding.

        1. History of involvement in community affairs.

        2. Past contributions in time, talent, and dollars to communities.

    B. G&T is a responsible neighbor.

        1. Campus-type vs. heavy industry.

        2. Absence of pollution problems—G&T recognizes environmental obligations.

        3. G&T assumes responsibility for most of its own needs—waste disposal, snow plowing, security, etc.

        4. The company is convinced that abutter's property values will increase as a result of G&T's presence.

IV. G&T as a developer and owner of property

    A. G&T has the technical competence to excel in the task of land development.

        1. It uses the best architectural talents available.

        2. Its past architectural accomplishments indicate the importance the company places on its development skills.

    B. G&T has a reputation not only for initial quality, but also for continuing concern: upkeep, maintenance, and improvement are equally important to our employees and to our neighbors.

    C. The advantages of dealing with a single developer, rather than several are important to a community (control, efficiency, simplicity, etc.)

V. Our plan for development of the Fairlawn Park site

    A. Final appearance of site: showing of model—include all aspects, explain significant characteristics of the plan.

    B. Types and quality of construction.

        1. Buildings: density, use.

        2. Roads: access, egress.

        3. Landscaping: use of natural features.

    C. Impact on immediate environment.

        1. Favorable impact on remainder of park and any abutters.

2. Absence of environmental depletion or abuse.

3. Impact on traffic flow.

D. Schedule and cost.

1. When (after selection) construction would begin; how quickly it would progress; when it would be concluded. (Mention temporary inconvenience during construction.)

2. G&T Company's projected investment in the site.

3. Possible long-range expansion at Fairlawn.

VI. Economic impact: benefits vs. costs

A. Benefits to Oaktown.

1. Tax contribution.

a. History of taxes paid to other communities.

b. Estimated annual tax to be paid by G&T.

2. Favorable effects on local business and services.

3. G&T employment potential.

a. Long-range steady growth.

b. Wide diversity of customers.

B. Costs to Oaktown are minimal, especially in comparison to other types of development (e.g., residential).

1. Nearly all costs of development will be borne by G&T. Exceptions:

a. Some road construction.

b. Streetlights.

2. Continuing costs to Oaktown would be few and small.

a. Negligible impact on schools.

b. Small (or no) requirement for local services such as roads, utilities, police and fire services, snow removal, waste collection.

C. In sum: many economic benefits, few economic costs.

The G&T expanded outline reflects decisions carefully made to bring purpose and emphasis to a collection of random information; but, of course, that outline is not the only way to organize the presentation. You probably already have suggestions for improvement, and that makes sense. Each of us views information from a different perspective and with different values. It is possible that a major point for one person is not worth air time for someone else. Differences in how we perceive the audience, differences in objectives—even differences in the time available for the presentation—will affect the outline. Organizing information, like communication itself, is not a science; it is a craft.

Next, we will explore some of the important patterns of organization and examine the differences between telling and selling.

## EXPOSITION OR PERSUASION?

It is useful to think of presentations as falling into two classes:

*Expository:* A presentation in which the objective is simply to impart information to an audience.

*Persuasive:* A presentation in which the objective requires persuading the audience to support a program or take a course of action. This type of presentation relies to a large extent on logical arguments.

Of course, pure examples of either class are rare. Almost every presentation is a mix of argument and information. But separating the expository and persuasive elements can help you recognize the special patterns of organization each uses. Knowing the patterns will allow you to be consistent in how you use them.

## EXPOSITORY PATTERNS

When the objective is to give the audience some information, then your presentation can use one of these organizational patterns.

*Chronology:* This pattern involves the relating of a series of events in time sequence. This pattern is simple to use, but be careful to include only events that are important to the overall exposition. The most common error is the omission of an important event.

*Analysis:* From the Greek *ana lien,* to break asunder, analysis is the breaking of your subject into parts and explaining each part in turn. Analysis is frequently used for technical presentations in which one must discuss parts, assemblies, systems, and phases. Analysis is a divide-and-conquer method that can work well.

*Classification:* The partner of analysis; classification is the collecting of items with certain common qualities into categories. Classification is a potent tool. It brings logical order to a presentation. It simplifies explanations and makes them easier for an audience to grasp and retain. Employees, for example, can be classified any number of ways, such as: Male/female; Hourly-paid/weekly-paid/monthly-paid; Production/professional/clerical/trades/managerial. Managerial employees can be further classified as: Supervisory/middle-management/executive.

*Cause and effect:* As you might expect, cause and effect is a mainstay of business presentations. We are always explaining "How we got into this fix." Cause and effect has a dual nature. We can start with causes, and explain the effects they produce, or start with effects and trace back to their causes.

*Question and answer:* What is the first thing the audience needs to know? the second? the third? and so forth. Question and answer consists of posing each question and then answering it. Consider using Q.&A. organization whenever your presentation requires explaining a body of information to an audience. The rules for Q.&A. require empathy for your audience. Begin with the first question in the mind of your audience. Next, imagine you have answered it. What question next requires answering? The two precautions to be aware of are: 1) be certain that *every* question your audience may have gets asked and answered; 2) be sure that the questions are raised in the order that satisfies the needs of your audience.

Expository presentations are by no means rare, and the higher one's perch in the organization tree the greater the need becomes for information. (A corporation president, for example, needs to possess an astonishing range of facts in order to make informed decisions.) Usually the expository presentation is triggered by that need, which comes in the form of a question, such as: "What is the problem with (X) and what are we doing about it?"; "What do this year's capital expenditures look like?"; "How is the new product coming along?"; "Are we competitive with our employee benefits?"; or, "What is our research division working on?" Very often, the question itself can set the organizational pattern of the presentation. The first question above can be answered by a presentation that:

1. Provides a detailed description of the problem
2. Reviews the available solutions
3. Explains why you chose the solution you did
4. Provides a current situation report
5. Projects when the "problem" will be solved

Answering question two requires analysis: capital expenditures broken into facilities and equipment, each in turn broken into smaller segments. Question three requires a progress report. Typically, the organization requires a review of problems overcome, problems being solved, and prospects for timely availability of the new product. Question four calls for a presentation with a simple organization—a benefit-by-benefit *comparison* between us and other specific companies (or a community average). For question five (which is trickier because it is a general question), classification might work best. Organize the presentation around *categories* of work (hardware, software) or *disciplines* (optical, electronic, chemical). Another approach is *organizational.* Explain the major work in progress by each group in the research division.

In each case, the organizational pattern reflects the original question that prompted the presentation. If the question is vague, do not hesitate to get a more specific version. You could be organizing an answer to the wrong question!

## PERSUASIVE PATTERNS: LOGIC

Most business presentations require persuasion. Objectives typically involve convincing other people to approve a purchase, fund a program, adopt a new policy, prevent an action from being carried out, or even maintain the status quo. The basic difference is that of *advocacy.* In a persuasive presentation, you must organize the facts into logical arguments. The audience should be aware of your position at the outset and you should expect your arguments to be questioned. But your *logic* need never be questioned. The rules of logic evolved many centuries ago, and the patterns of logical argument are as valid today as they were in Aristotle's time. You need to be familiar with just three patterns of logic: *deduction, induction,* and *elimination.*

### Deduction

With *deduction,* you begin with a statement, (major premise) that every audience member must accept as true and then proceed to build a conclusion, using that beginning statement as a foundation. For example:

*Major premise:* All customer returns have been for incorrect wiring of the tuning circuit.

*Minor premise:* All wiring of the tuning circuit is performed by production line five.

*Conclusion:* Production line five has caused all customer returns.

Remember that when you use the deductive pattern, your audience *must* accept your major premise. In real situations, it is often necessary to prove your opening statement with indisputable evidence whenever that statement is not self-evident. Be especially careful of seemingly universal (but mushy) truths, such as "All employees are seeking self-fulfillment." In deduction, the major premise must withstand every test of truth; if it does not, the whole structure crumbles and falls.

### Induction

In the *inductive* pattern, an accumulation of specific facts builds to a general conclusion, for example:

1. Of our fifteen products, only the Modulator is unprofitable.
2. The Modulator is a complex, outdated design being overwhelmed in the market by a less expensive, more reliable import.
3. The customer returns of Modulators is 7 percent, highest of all our products.
4. We have enough Modulators in inventory for ten months' sales.
5. Modulator production workers are needed to help make other products that are backordered.

Therefore, we should stop producing Modulators as quickly as possible.

This accumulation of facts supports the conclusion and allows the so-called inductive leap. Before making that leap, however, the audience must be convinced that the overwhelming weight of facts supports the conclusion and only *that* conclusion. This example is unusual in that every fact supports the conclusion. In real situations, the facts are hardly ever so one-sided, and you must prove why *on balance* your conclusions are correct.

### Elimination

The third persuasive pattern calls for listing all the alternatives, then disposing of them one by one until the audience is left with either the best course of action or the most likely cause of a problem.

This approach sounds simple, but elimination has its pitfalls. To begin with, you must list *every* reasonable alternative (or *cause* if you are isolating the source of a problem). Few things can be as devastating as the question, "Have you considered _____ ?" and your only answer must be, "No, that wasn't considered in our analysis."

Next, you must slay all the dragons but one, which is not always easy to do. Sometimes dragons get resurrected by uncooperative audiences or alas, your surviving dragon also has a fatal flaw to be pointed out by an especially astute and helpful audience member.

## SOME CONCLUDING THOUGHTS ABOUT PERSUASION: EMOTIONS

In the previous section, we discussed the patterns of organization that apply to persuasive presentations. Persuasion is an arrangement of facts that appeals to our sense of logic. It would be short-sighted, however, not to mention that it is not always pure logic that persuades us.

We are creatures of emotion as well as intellect. Sometimes the most logical argument imaginable will not convince an audience that your cause or your course is right. Why? Because it doesn't "feel" right. Audiences often must be moved to action in spite of all your reasoning. Presentations, after all, usually propose change. Most people do not like change; they find it threatening.

The list of emotional factors that can affect the outcome of a presentation is as long as human experience itself. As we touch on a few of the most important of these nonlogical factors, remember to be aware of them not just as potential obstructions, but also as powerful allies in the process of persuasion.

### Fear

An emotion with an undeservedly poor reputation, fear can be a healthy motivator. We use other words to describe this emotion, of course. We are "concerned" that profits are slumping, for example, or a bit "apprehensive" about the reliability of the latest design. Whatever the terminology, if the situation warrants it, we can either *act* out of fear or, curiously, be *paralyzed* by it.

### Gain

The desire to gain is often the force that moves entire organizations as well as individuals. It is naïve to assume that audience members do not view any proposal in the light of personal as well as organizational gain. As a rule, the higher one's position, the more one's personal goals become identified with those of the organization.

Incidentally, it is a mistake always to clothe the desire for gain with the the cloak of greed. Lincoln wanted the power of the American presidency; Ghandi wanted to gain independence for India; Saint Francis of Assisi wanted to establish a religious order. Wanting to gain an increased share of the pantyhose market is by no means so lofty a goal, but neither is it to be scorned.

The other side of the gain equation is *avoidance of loss*. Once having achieved something, we tend to want to hold on to it. Loss avoidance, in fact, is one of the most common themes of business presentations.

### The Herd Instinct

Most of us see ourselves as independent thinkers; but organizations consist of group activities, and being out of step can be intensely uncomfortable. Examples:

Mr. Bullard, our car is the only one on the market without front disc brakes.

Our employees are the only ones in the industry without medical coverage.

### Testimonial

Testimonials can have a strong, persuasive influence in business presentations. You may not care which athlete eats what breakfast cereal, but you may be influenced by the judgments, or even the opinions, of someone whose proven expertise and credibility on the subject at hand are outstanding. Of course, citing a prominent, highly placed, and influential member of your organization as an enthusiastic supporter of your proposal is mere name dropping—a shabby practice that practically no one condones, but almost everyone employs.

### Other Emotional Factors

The range of human emotions produces a wide variety of responses in communication. We all share a sense of pride and possess a measure of competitiveness and compassion. Most of us enjoy a challenge, take risks, and seek recognition and acceptance. In the last analysis, these seemingly nonlogical factors can often tip the balance scales one way or another. A successful presenter is always aware of their presence, is always aware that logic alone does not rule the human will. If it did, Sir Edmund Hillary would never have climbed Mount Everest.

## THE ENDING

The most important key to a presentation's ending is *do not waste it*. We tend to remember the beginnings and endings of things. The ending of a presentation represents an opportunity, not just the point when you stop talking.

How you construct the ending depends largely on the subject and your objective. In a highly expository presentation, it is important to summarize each section as you go along. The conclusion can be a brief summary of the main points and some suggestions on how to get more information or how to apply the newly acquired knowledge. In a persuasive presentation the ending is a last bid to achieve your objective. Use it to summarize your chief arguments or conclusions. If appropriate, give an especially telling example of the problem or stress the consequences of not adopting your proposal. And by all means include a hook.

The *hook* is the next step in the process of reaching your objective. Remember, the presentation is never an end in itself; it is a vehicle for achieving that end. What happens *after* the presentation is more important than the presentation itself. A hook can take an infinite variety of forms, including the suggestion to approve a proposal, purchase, or program; establish a steering committee; agree to attend a follow-up meeting; sanction a report; approve further study; or, agree to give the presentation to another group. The closing section of a persuasive presentation should contain such a hook. *You* should provide it. If the next step is not obvious, create a logical follow-up. Each presentation has but one ending; don't squander it.

## OUTLINE WITH THREE-BY-FIVE-INCH CARDS

Try preparing your outline on 3-by-5-inch index cards. This practice will afford you much more flexibility than using sheets of paper. The method is especially helpful in organizing large presentations. Begin by writing the main theme and all the supporting themes on a single card (use a five-by-seven-inch card if you need more space). Next, write each supporting theme on a separate card (see Figure 2).

Each supporting theme (S.T.) is a *major topic* of your presentation. Next, work on the subtopics under each major topic. This time, list each subtopic at the top of the card, then jot down the supportive items for each subtopic. The first draft of the outline should look something like the format shown in Figure 3.

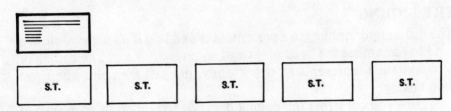

**Figure 2** Main Theme and Supporting Themes

You can now look at the entire plan of your presentation and make changes painlessly; thus:

*Material selection:* Eliminate cards or add new ones to fill in gaps in the flow.

*Topics:* Raise a subtopic card to major topic status. Each supporting statement then becomes a subtopic and gets written on a new card.

*Sequence:* You can change the order of the subtopics by simply moving individual cards or change the sequence of major topics by shifting the vertical rows of cards.

Once you are satisfied with the outline, *number* the cards in proper sequence and gather them up. The information on the cards can then be transcribed onto paper either for review by other people or for your own use in preparing a script.

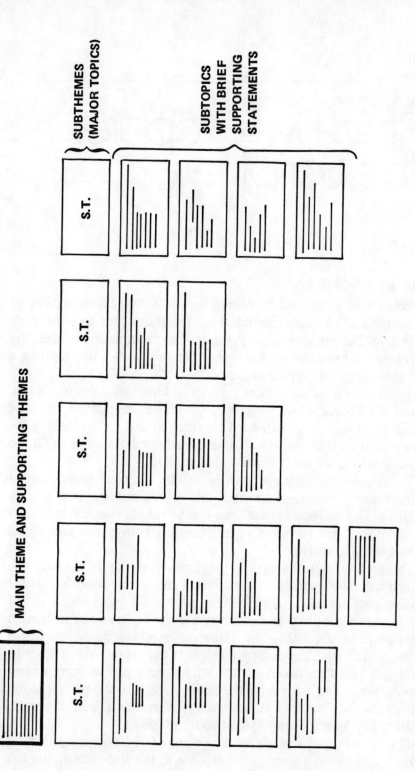

**Figure 3** Final Outline

# 6
# Step Five: Prepare the Script

**WHAT IS A SCRIPT?**

An audiovisual presentation, remember, is a two-channel form of communication, a series of sounds and images designed to accomplish an objective. The more carefully you plan those sounds and images, the more likely the presentation will succeed in its purpose. By preparing a script, you commit that plan to paper.

A common mistake is thinking only in terms of slides or visuals. As soon as we become aware that we must give a presentation, many of us begin rummaging through our files (mental and metal) looking for ideas for visuals. Once we have accumulated enough visuals to fill the allotted time, we are ready for the presentation.

The opposite approach is to write out the complete speech part of the presentation and then go back and figure out the best way to illustrate it. This method at least has a planned audio channel; but in my view, it still is not as effective as planning both audio and visual channels simultaneously.

Think of a script as a kind of program sheet that details what the audience will hear and see. A convenient and widely used format for preparing a script is shown in Figure 4. Rule an 8½ by 11-inch sheet of paper into two columns as shown in Figure 4. The column labeled *Audio* should be wider than the *Visual* column because more space is needed to write what the audience will hear than is needed to describe what it will see. This two-column format forces you to think in two channels. While you are writing the audio portion of the message, you must also create the visual information that will best illustrate, reinforce, highlight, or amplify that audio message.

The basic unit of a script is called a *frame*. A frame consists of all the vocal and visual information available to the audience during the

| AUDIO | VISUAL |
|---|---|
| 1. Purpose of today's meeting is not to tell each of you what your salary grade is, but to give you an overview of the Company's New Salary Program. | 1. Our new Salary Program<br><br>. . . an overview |
| 2. Here's what we'll cover . . .<br>First, a brief background; why did we need a new salary plan? How was it designed? Next, a description of the new plan, followed by an explanation of how it operates. Then, I'll do my best to answer any questions you may have. | 2. Agenda:<br>—Background<br>—Description of the plan<br>—How the plan operates<br>—Discussion/Questions |
| 3. To begin with, the old salary system had several inadequacies. It lived a shadowy existence. It was never corporately administered. It was vague and not understood. No method existed for evaluating jobs, and this led to a noticeable lack of consistency among divisions. These problems caused a growing awareness of the need to review and formalize a salary plan. | 3. Background:<br>—Inadequacies of the old plan<br>—Not a formal company system<br>—Vague - not understood<br>—No provision for evaluating jobs<br>—No consistency |
| 4. We needed a system whose structure would truly reflect the value of the jobs — when compared with each other and with the outside world. We needed a system everyone could easily understand. We also needed the methods to apply it uniformly. So much for defining the needs — how then, do we fulfill them? | 4. Needed: A salary program that is . . .<br>—Consistent - internally<br>—Competitive - externally<br>—Easily understood<br>—Uniformly administered |

**Figure 4** A Sample Script

projection of one slide, or *visual*. In the sample script, notice that horizontal lines are used to separate the frames. Notice, too, that when the visual is a word slide (or *simple* table), the actual words or tables are used in the script. In general, pictures and complex graphic visuals are not duplicated, but are simply described in the script.

How long should a frame be? The obvious answer is, "as long as necessary to make the points required." In practice, however, most advertising, marketing, or motivational presentations have short average frame spans. Typical frame durations run from one to ten seconds; but in business presentations, the frames are usually longer because the emphasis is on exposition and carefully structured argument rather than on creating a mood or spirit or conveying a series of impressions.

By working in frames, you build both audio and visual channels concurrently. However, each channel must be explained in turn. The next section will describe in detail how to prepare the audio channel; the following section will cover the range of visuals available to you and explain the techniques for creating effective (and avoiding ineffective) visuals. It is important, however, to remember that in practice, audio and visual channels are created simultaneously.

## CREATING THE AUDIO CHANNEL

### A Good Script Communicates

How many English languages exist today? If you think just one, you probably haven't heard two molecular biologists discussing the chemical bonds of protein molecules, or two computer specialists discussing the intricacies of a ballistics tracking program, or a group of investment analysts exchanging opinions on the latest market trends. Moreover, special languages are not solely the property of highly trained professionals. We all use them when we talk about not only our jobs, but also our special interests, hobbies, or activities. When CB radio fans "read the mail," they listen to the radio traffic without transmitting. "Low profile clinchers (tires) with high-pressure tubes and prestas (valves)" is a common expression to a serious cyclist. In Boston, an automobile traffic reporter is trying to create his own humorous traffic-jam language with such terms as "ramp cramp," "lane sprain," "grumper-to-grumper traffic," and "gawker blocker." The profusion of special languages is endless.

A special language uses English as a base and *jargon* to convey the special, exclusive meanings. Jargon is not a negative word, although some dictionaries are beginning to define jargon as "any unintelligible language." On the contrary, jargon is simply the special language of a profession, activity, or occupation. Jargon saves time and will always be with us. The problem with jargon is its exclusivity. It is language for *insiders*.

Communication requires breaching the walls that separate people. The word communication itself derives from the Latin *communes:* to *share* or to *make common*. We can communicate with each other only on the basis of what we *share*. You can communicate with an audience only on the basis of what you possess *in common* with that audience. The language of communication is simple and familiar. It makes no attempt to impress other people with ponderous and learned phrases. As Tom Anastasi, a friend and skilled communicator, says, "Impress people with your *ideas*, not your vocabulary!"

No matter how careful we are, however, we eventually all make the false assumption that we are communicating with an audience. Recently, when explaining to a group of executives how jargon saves words for insiders, I used the following example:

*Jargon:* Is a 1939D BU Jefferson really worth $60.00?

*"Plain" English:* Is a Jefferson nickel, minted in 1939 at the Denver Mint, and which has never been circulated and is in bright and unmarked condition, really worth $60.00?

I explained that the insiders—in this case, the numismatists—could communicate much more efficiently using jargon. Then came the humbling event we all need to keep our perspective: one member of the audience asked me, "What's a numismatist?"

For communicating via the audio channel of presentation, bear in mind these simple rules as you prepare your script:

- Avoid the *unnecessary* use of jargon. Use a language familiar to your audience.

- If you must use unfamiliar terms, *define* them as you introduce them.

- Be especially wary of *acronyms* and *abbreviations*. They are simply short forms of jargon.

- Be concerned with *level of detail*. How much supportive and amplifying information does your audience need? Too little will be confusing, too much will be tedious.

- Never keep an audience in suspense. Come to the point. Explain your objectives. Suspense is wonderful for detective stories, but it usually irritates an audience of business people or technical people.

- In general, never emphasize the differences between you and your audience; always deal in the similarities. (I'm reminded of the story of the man who began his speech to the Daughters of the American Revolution with the following statement: "As a life-long left-wing liberal democrat, I'd like to explain my views on welfare.")

Other important aspects of the audio channel include: style, pace, balance, unity, and emphasis.

### The Importance of Style

Always remember that you are writing a speech. Your speech should sound like *you* do when you speak naturally. Use simple, familiar, precise expression. Do not be afraid to be yourself. If the audio channel of your presentation sounds like a written report, at least two bad things will happen. First, you will need to memorize all the fancy language, which is not easy. Second, if you cannot memorize it, you will have to read it. That's doubly deadly, not only because the overly formal language puts audiences to sleep, but also because you should *never read anything* to an audience; it bores them to distraction. A good way to avoid this trap is to dictate your words (following your outline, of course) and then have the recording transcribed onto paper. You can then edit the typed version, polishing and eliminating any confusing or ambiguous passages.

*Style* really means the way *you* express yourself: your manner, your voice, your words, not those of Winston Churchill or Orson Welles, but the essential you! One key to successful presentations is simply to be yourself, but be as good as you can be.

Be aware of the *tone* of your words. It is possible unintentionally to communicate an enormous range of impressions to an audience. One's words can seem sarcastic, aloof, paternalistic, defensive, grave, condescending, academic, or too chummy, to cite just a few possible tones. The tone may also be neutral. The important thing is to avoid extremes and to be certain that the tone is appropriate to your subject, to your relationship with that specific audience, and to the situation.

### *Humor*

The tone of a presentation can be humorous. In fact, there is a persistent belief that *every* presentation must at least begin and end with a joke. (A joke puts everyone at ease and gets the attention of the audience.) Use humor when it is appropriate, but also be aware of several pitfalls.

If you use humor, it should be funny to *every* member of your audience. This is not always easy to do; and, of course, you *already* have ruled out ethnic, sexist, and bawdy humor. Be sensitive to the possible reactions of everyone. Example:

Apart from that, did you enjoy the play, Mrs. Lincoln?

Your first reaction to that classic one-liner may be hearty laughter. Your second reaction could be a tinge of remorse. Perhaps to some people, it is not at all amusing. Again, how many people who survived the horrors of Nazi prison camps can enjoy the humor of "Hogan's Heros"?

When writing a humorous tone into your presentation, remember these four rules:

*Rule number one: Humor should be universal.*

*Rule number two: Do not be a stand-up comic.* If your script contains one gag after another, your audience may be rolling on the floor with laughter, but they will not be getting the message; they will be waiting for the next punch line. Use humor in a presentation the way you use spices in a meal—sparingly, to accent the basic flavor.

*Rule number three: Avoid clumsy or self-deprecating humor.* It is a bad idea to characterize yourself or your associates as louts, boobs, or just plain folks for the sake of humor, yet it is done endlessly. Generally, no person or group should be the target of your humor.

*Rule number four: Examine your delivery style.* A few people simply lack the expression, the animation, the sense of timing needed to use humor effectively. If your delivery style isn't suited to it, don't use humor. Few things are as deadly, for example, as a presentation that begins with a vain attempt to get a laugh. The silence (or groans or weak tittering) makes your audience uncomfortable and puts you in a deep hole at the outset.

## The Importance of Pace

As you prepare your script, be aware of the clock. Think of the audience's ability to absorb new ideas and their ramifications. Are you giving them enough time? Conversely, are you dawdling—using too much time to make a relatively simple point? The term *idea density* was coined by William Gallagher, an authority on human communication, to describe the flow of ideas and their supporting structure. Strive to tailor the idea density, to pace your presentation, to your audience's ability to process the material.

### The Importance of Unity

In a business or technical presentation, a frame is the rough equivalent of the paragraph in writing. Thus, each frame should be unified; that is, designed to make a point, to make a statement and support it. Ask yourself, "What is the point of this frame?" "Have I strayed from the point by introducing unrelated information?" "Am I trying to make more than one *major point* with this frame?" (If so, use more than one frame.) And finally, "Have I developed the point fully?"

### The Importance of Emphasis

The frame is emphatic when it makes its point convincingly, forcefully. We tend to remember the beginnings and the ends of things. Just as with the beginning and ending of the entire presentation, concentrate on how each frame starts and concludes. It often helps to state the point at the outset and then to use the frame to illustrate or support it. If you are using induction, list and explain the facts that support the conclusion to be driven home at the end of the frame.

Transitions help to provide both emphasis and coherence. They reinforce points and can help an audience prepare for the next step. A linkage at the start or end of a frame can put the whole frame in perspective. Examples of transitions:

So much for the benefits of the new system; how about the fixed and variable costs?

So much for the design features of the Model 7L11; how can we produce it efficiently?

Of all these alternatives, one promises the greatest return with the least risk: Manual Assembly. Here's why.

Use transitions to link the larger sections of your presentation. With a brief summary, let the audience know that you are concluding the discussion of a major topic, then, with an introductory link, prepare the way for the next section. On the visual side, one of the most useful devices for achieving emphasis through transitions is the agenda slide. Shown near the beginning of the presentation, it simply lists the subjects to be covered. The same slide is repeated at the beginning of each subject, but with the subject at hand highlighted in some way. This technique has the advantage of emphasizing: 1) what you have covered; 2) what you are about to discuss next; and 3) what remains to be covered. This is called the "you-are-here" slide.

A good script uses a variety of devices to achieve emphasis. *Repetition* is one useful method, not dull reiteration, but careful reinforcement of one channel by the other or thoughtful restatement from various perspectives. So, too, is *illustration* or *example.* Emphasis often can be achieved with *analogy* (an extended comparison between two things, such as the flow of electricity and the flow of water) or *metaphor,* "in the cell, the ribosome is the *factory* for building amino acids." Emphasis makes a presentation memorable.

### Helpful Hints on Writing the Audio Channel of Your Script

- *Don't Put It Off*—A good script is a thoughtful construction of words and images. Writing requires care and craftsmanship and takes time. If you wait until the eleventh hour, the price of delay will be paid in the quality of the presentation.

- *Follow Your Outline*—After expending all that energy to organize your material, it's now payday. It would be sheer folly not to cash in. But do not follow an outline slavishly. Begin anywhere you feel comfortable, anywhere your familiarity or interest in the material will make it easier to get started. Save the difficult sections for mop-up operations later when you have completed most of the work.

- *Put Yourself in Your Audience's Shoes*—Empathy is the key to effective communication. Write every word with the needs of your audience foremost in your mind. Try to become your audience as you create the script.

- *Think Visually as You Write*—Remember that *two* channels must carry the message. As you prepare the audio portion of your script, always consider the best way to use the visual channel in order to make your point or to carry the burden of exposition. Be aware of its special power to illustrate, reinforce, make immediate, and enliven your material.

All of these hints provide a timely cue to introduce the subject of visuals.

## CREATING THE VISUAL CHANNEL

In broadest terms, a *visual* is anything that requires the eyes of an audience to focus its attention. Visuals are useful for both audience and presenter. For the audience, they provide a series of road signs to highlight the content and aid in remembering the key ideas of the presentation. Visuals can contribute supporting detail, provide emphasis, and add vitality to dry material. They can be used to explain or clarify concepts at a glance where words alone would take much more time. One classic example of this last point is the diagram shown in Figure 5, used to explain the Pythagorean theorum.

For the presenter, the visual provides the cues—the trigger words, phrases, and images—that can help the speaker get through the presentation without reading notes or cue cards. This in turn allows the presenter to spend more time in contact with the audience.

Visual media can be conveniently divided into two classes:

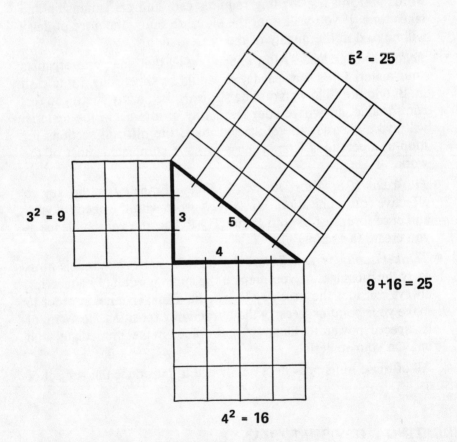

**Figure 5** Explaining the Pythagorean Theorum

| **Nonprojected** | **Projected** |
|---|---|
| Chalkboard (blackboard) | Overhead transparencies |
| Easel pad | 35-mm slides |
| Flip charts | Lantern slides |
| Models | Opaque projection |
| Handouts | Videotape playback |
| The real object | Movies |
| (Others) | (Others) |

One decision you must make for every presentation you do is, "Which visual medium best suits *this* situation?" Let me help with that decision by explaining the strengths and drawbacks of each medium.

## Nonprojected Media

### *Chalkboard*

A chalkboard is the least satisfying of the nonprojected media because the presenter must *create* the visual during the presentation. Writing on the board requires turning away from your audience for long periods. Unless you perfect the technique of writing (or drawing) without blocking your audience's view of the chalkboard, you must cope with the problem of maintaining contact by using your voice alone. Creating the visual channel takes time, time that can be better spent in other ways. On the plus side, the chalkboard is inexpensive (provided you have one available) and quite flexible in that you can write, add detail, change, and erase at will.

### *Easel Pad*

An easel pad is a large (usually nineteen-by-twenty-four-inch) pad of paper mounted on an easel. The advantage of the easel pad is that the visual (or artwork) can be prepared in advance. The presenter simply turns the page to show the next visual. If the presenter uses the pad to draw or write on during the presentation, the advantage is lost. The easel pad then becomes a paper chalkboard. The easel pad has other advantages; it is relatively inexpensive, flexible, and easy to use. The disadvantages are its small size, which rules it out for large audiences (more than about twenty people). Also, the easel pad has an informal quality that can make it ill-suited to highly formal presentations.

### Flip Charts

Flip charts are stiff cardboard sheets (usually Bainbridge Board) on which artwork is printed and drawn. They can be cut to any size, although the most common size is twenty-by-forty inches. Flip charts may be used with a variety of easels, some of which have binding rings for small visuals.

One advantage of flip charts is their usefulness in informal presentations where projection equipment is unavailable, unworkable, or undesirable. Flip charts work best with small audiences (fifteen or fewer people). Occasionally you may need to show an accumulation of visuals to an audience, leaving each one "up," or visible as you progress. Flip charts work well in such a situation. So does the easel pad; incidentally, if you are willing to tear the sheets from the pad, then tape them to the wall.

Flip charts also have several disadvantages. They are seldom desirable for presentations for several reasons. First, the expensive artwork is applied directly to the chart, then it goes into combat. It is too easy to scuff, smudge, damage, or even lose. It is preferable to reproduce the artwork in a projected medium. One can always replace a slide as long as the original art is intact. Second, flip charts, especially the large ones, are cumbersome to transport and often awkward to use. Third, they do not work well with large audiences. Fourth, they do not lend themselves to easy reproduction in reduced format. An overhead transparency, for example, can project the same amount of information as a flip chart, but on a large screen.

### Models

Models are useful for replicating a large object on a smaller scale, such as machines, buildings, floor plans, and roadways. The presentation can use the actual model and/or photographs of it for large audiences. Models usually are limited to presentations in which the stakes are high enough to justify the considerable expense of building them.

### Handouts

Technically handouts are things you put in the hands of your audience, such as an object or a piece of paper containing information.

Handouts can be used as visuals during a presentation, but they do have disadvantages. First, it takes time to distribute the handout. You need to find ways of holding your audience's attention and introducing the handout during distribution. (Ask for volunteers to pass out the material while you spend your time preparing the audience for it.) Second, the mere presence of the handout is a distraction. Audience members will want to examine it and extract information at their own pace, which means that your words will not reach most of them. The best way to deal with this problem is to give the audience a little time to get familiar with the handout before you begin to discuss it. Allow a little intellectual play before beginning the work of exposition. Then you must carefully guide your audience through the handout as if it were any other kind of visual.

The second and most common use of handouts is to give the audience a record of the presentation for later reference. This second application should not be confused with using a handout as a visual. If you wish to provide reference material, distribute it *after* the presentation is over, when it will not distract your audience.

### The Real Object

Depending on the circumstances, you can use anything in the environment as a visual, including field trips, plant tours, and equipment demonstrations. Several problems must be considered, however: 1) getting your audience to and from the site; 2) narrowing their attention to the specific details you wish to present; 3) the presence of distractions in the environment, such as high noise levels; and 4) physical limitations of the environment. For example, the space that the audience must occupy may be so small that only a veteran U-boat captain can concentrate. (Apart from sheer olfactory considerations, the larger the audience, the more likely it is that people will not be able to *see* what you wish to show them.) The real object can be effective as a visual, sometimes dramatically so, but be sensitive to possible logistical and physical problems.

### Projected Media

Most business and technical presentations use projected images for several reasons. Projected images:

- Are better suited to large audiences
- Permit more control over the visual channel than most nonprojected media
- Tend to communicate a higher degree of formality
- Allow for more audience contact by the presenter, when used properly

### The Overhead Transparency

The overhead transparency (or Vu-Graph) is the most widely used medium for business and technical presentations for several reasons:

- The projectors are easy to obtain, and the machines for making visuals are usually within easy reach in most companies.

- The speaker can face the audience and use the transparency as a cue card. There is no need to look at the screen. The speaker can devote more time to making contact with the audience.

- The room does not have to be darkened. This allows interaction between speaker and audience (and helps to keep people awake!). It also lets people take notes.

- The overhead transparency is an 8½-by-11-inch acetate sheet. The usual field size, or information area on the transparency, is about seven-by-nine inches. That means one can project much more information with an overhead transparency than with any other projection method, except the opaque projector. Although it is *not* a good idea to pack information into any visual, the overhead transparency does have a distinct edge in presentations that require complex visuals.

- The projector is at the speaker's side, which permits a measure of control over the visual. The speaker can point to key features, mask and gradually uncover information, use overlays to add information, and mark on the visual with a grease pencil. The presenter can easily switch the projector off to focus the audience's attention on the speaker and the audio channel alone. Of course, a similar effect can be achieved with 35-mm and lantern slides by using an opaque slide, but the room lights must be turned up by an assistant, which seems less spontaneous and a bit contrived.

- Overhead transparencies are inexpensive and easy to make.

- Because they can be made quickly, overhead transparencies allow last-minute changes. Thirty-five mm and lantern slides require much longer turnaround times to produce.

- Overhead transparencies may be reproduced on office copiers for use as handouts.

This is an impressive list of advantages, but overhead transparencies also have some drawbacks. In fact, sometimes the advantages can be liabilities:

- Because the visuals are in front of the speaker, it is easy to use them as a crutch. Simply reading slides without adding further information not only wastes the audio channel, but also bores the audience and makes the speaker seem passive.

- The ability to control the visuals can backfire if the speaker constantly fiddles with the visuals, points to everything in sight, or wastes time underlining or circling things unnecessarily.

- Overhead transparencies can be made to project blocks of solid colors; but in practice, color is expensive and bothersome.

- In order to reach large audiences, the screen must be elevated and tipped forward to eliminate the keystone effect, a distortion in which the top of the projected image is wider than the bottom. In fact, avoiding this problem requires careful planning; sometimes it cannot be avoided.

- With small groups, the speaker can easily block the view of the screen for a few audience members. Allowing all audience members to see the screen requires careful placement of both the screen and the speaker. One way to avoid blocking the screen is for the speaker to remain seated; but a speaker should not sit. To maintain control and leadership, you should stand, if at all possible. (More on screen placement later.)

- Because of their limited use of color, their inability to use continuous tone—or photographic—images, and their semiformal style, overhead transparencies are not as effective in highly formal presentations, especially with large audiences.

On the whole, however, with proper preparation and effective delivery techniques, the assets of overhead transparencies outweigh the liabilities. Two types of overhead projectors are available: the transmission and the reflection type (see Figure 6).

The transmission type is larger, much less portable, and it uses a fan, which gives off heat and noise that may be annoying to those sitting close to it. The reflection type is more portable, silent, but will project a double image if the visual does not lie quite flat. Also, the reflector plate tends to get scratched easily, and the scratches show on the screen. Replacing the reflector plate is expensive.

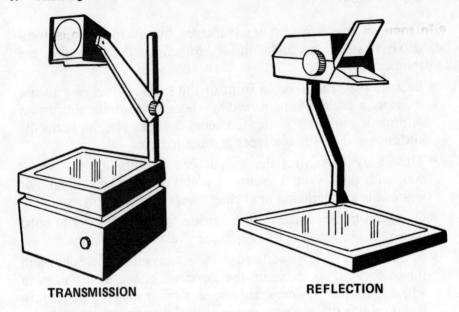

**TRANSMISSION**                    **REFLECTION**

**Figure 6** Two Types of Overhead Projector

### *35-mm Slides*

Thirty-five mm comes in a close second in popularity for business presentations, and for some compelling reasons. Thirty-five mm (two-by-two-inch) slides are more stimulating than any medium mentioned thus far. The reason is that color photography of people, places, and things lends an air of drama and realism not available with overheads or with any of the nonprojected media. Color also lends interest and variety to the presentation of statistical or technical material. A presentation featuring 35-mm slides works best in formal presentations to large audiences, especially when the subject is not too complex.

This medium does have a few disadvantages, however:

- Thirty-five mm slides are comparatively expensive—not the relatively minor expense of color processing, but the major expense of color artwork.

- The field size of 35-mm is comparatively small; only about eight lines of type should be used on a single slide. Diagrams and charts must be simple. Thirty-five mm does not lend itself to complexity.

- The dramatic and arresting qualities of 35-mm slides tend to draw most of audience's attention, reducing the speaker to a secondary role. This, of course, can be an advantage for the untrained or infrequent speaker.

- In some organizations, 35-mm slides may be frowned on as too "show biz" for business presentations, especially for small audiences (fifteen or fewer people).

- Slides require a darkened room. The speaker must work doubly hard to make contact with the audience, and the audience cannot take notes. These problems can be lessened, however, by using a room whose lights are controlled by a dimmer. It is possible to find a compromise light level that will allow the audience to take notes yet still see the visuals.

- The 35-mm projector is more complex mechanically than the overhead projector. Occasionally a slide may refuse to seat itself (hang up), and on rare occasions the machine can jam. In highly formal presentations, a skilled assistant must be available to provide first aid if needed. Incidentally, the assistant will probably have to control the room lights as well.

### Lantern Slides

Lantern slides are 3¼-by-4 inch, usually glass-encased transparencies. They have the same advantages as 35-mm slides, but their larger field size makes them better suited to more complex technical presentations. Lantern slides are often used with large audiences, especially at technical symposiums. They do have some disadvantages. The projector is larger and less portable than a 35-mm machine. Each slide must be manually loaded by an assistant *during* the presentation. Making the slides is a more involved and expensive process.

### The Opaque Projector

An opaque projector projects in color anything you can get into it, such as sheets of paper and even small, flat objects. But the projector is large, heavy, bulky, hot, noisy, and requires a darkened room.

### Videotapes and Movies

Videotapes and movies combine moving color images and sound —a potent mixture that can add realism, interest, and excitement to a presentation. Both media are "canned" forms of presentation. Although this book deals with live presentations, a quick summary of the canned variety is worthwhile.

Videotape is far less expensive and much easier to produce than are movies. The tapes can be erased and re-used. On the other hand, videotape is not suited to large audiences; the screen is too small. This problem can be overcome by using several monitors, but this is quite costly. Also remember that unless they are professionally produced, videotapes fall far short of broadcast quality. People are accustomed to seeing perfection on their home sets and may be disappointed with anything less.

Movies are prohibitively expensive to produce and to change should it be necessary. They do have the advantage of large projection size.

With any canned presentation, however, you must turn your audience over to the whirring, clicking machinery. Even though it may be useful to do so in order to show something especially relevant, keep it brief. Business audiences tend to react negatively if they think they are being entertained.

As a summary, Table 3 lists the visual formats discussed here and compares them by the most important criteria.

## Effective Visuals

### Choosing Effective Visuals

Once you have decided on the medium to convey the visual half of your message, you must continue to make choices. As you prepare your script, you must select, from all those available, the one type of visual that best communicates the point or message of each frame. You must keep asking, "What is the best way to explain, support, illustrate, emphasize, or reinforce this idea?"

The types of visuals you may choose include: words, diagrams, tables, schematics, "live" objects (models), mockups, graphs, maps, illustrations, photographs, and cartoons. We will discuss most of these types of visuals after first looking at the qualities that make *any* visual effective.

### General Rules for Effective Visuals

*Unity* means that each visual should make a single point. Dwell on that point for no more than two minutes.

*Simplicity* is the key to visuals that work. Avoid fancy artwork for the sake of being creative or artsy. This only dilutes the impact of the visual. Every line should have a function. The purpose of a visual is to make ideas and relationships simple and memorable. Color, too, should be functional and not merely decorative. Use plenty of blank space.

*Economy* means not adding one unnecessary word or number. The impact of the visual should stand out immediately, and not be hidden in

Table 3 Selecting a Visual Medium

| Medium | Cost | Portability | For Complex Visuals | Degree of Formality | Rough Size of Audience | Lead Time | Comments |
|---|---|---|---|---|---|---|---|
| Chalkboard | 0 | 0 | Fair | Poor | Up to 35 | 0 | Slow - cumbersome - poor audience contact |
| Easel Pad | Low | Poor | Poor | Poor | Up to 15 | Short | Good for small, informal, non-complex presentations |
| Flip Charts | Med. to High | Poor to Fair | Fair | Fair | Up to 15 | Med. to Long | Often cumbersome - expensive - small audiences |
| Models | Very High | Depends on Size | Very Good | Excellent | Up to 15 | Very long | Cost must be justified - can be highly effective |
| The Real Object | Depends | 0 | Very Good | Good | Up to 35 | 0 | Be aware of logistics and the environment |
| Overhead Transparencies | Med. | Fair to Good | Very Good | Good | Up to 50 | Short | Popular - inexpensive - quick - may become a "crutch" |
| 35MM Slides | Med. to High | Very Good | Poor to Fair | Excellent | Up to 400 | Med. | Color - flexibility - live photographs - small field size |
| Lantern Slides | Med. to High | Poor | Fair | Excellent | Up to 400 | Med. to long | Good for large groups and complex data |
| Opaque Projection | Low | Terrible | Very Good | Poor to Fair | Up to 35 | Short | Heavy, bulky, noisy, etc. OK for informal meetings |
| Videotape | Med. | Very Poor | Poor to Fair | Good to very good | Up to 15 | Short to Med. | Limited to small groups - inexpensive and flexible |
| Movies | Extremely High | Fair | Very Good | Excellent | Up to 400 | Very long | Potent visual tool, but with many drawbacks |

a thicket of details and supporting information. Remember, *the speaker provides the supporting details, not the visual.*

*Consistency* requires that the visuals use the same type style and art style. Scales should be consistent, too.

*Readability* means that letters should be no smaller than ¼-inch high on overhead transparencies. On the screen, letters must be 1¼-inches high to be easily read at a distance of thirty-five feet, 1¾-inches at forty-five feet, 2½-inches at fifty-five feet. Lines should be ¼ to ⅜ of an inch minimum thickness. Avoid black type on dark colored backgrounds (blue, purple, dark green). Use a bold typeface that is clean, i.e., letters without serifs. Many people prefer Univers or a typeface resembling it.

## THIS IS A SAMPLE OF UNIVERS BOLD TYPE

Avoid vertical lettering; it is difficult to read. Put the information as near the *top* of the visual as possible. Some people in the back rows will not be able to see the bottom of the screen. Use white letters on dark backgrounds. White on blue is especially effective. Again, use plenty of space; it helps readability.

Using a typewriter for making overhead transparencies is never easy, but it can be done. Begin by making sure the typewriter's font, or letters, are clean. *Always* use a carbon ribbon. The type style should be large, bold, and uncluttered. Gothic type styles work well, so does the Orator font in the IBM Selectric typewriter. The choice of paper is critical. *Avoid standard bond paper;* its surface is too rough for sharp, dense, unbroken letters. Use a twenty-pound sulfite paper, which has no rag content. Office copy machine paper (used in plain-paper office copiers) is satisfactory, but not as good. Be sure that the typewriter's impression control is set to give the best results.

*Clarity* is important. The audience should be able to grasp the main idea of the visual in no more than fifteen to twenty seconds. Do not give your audience ugly riddles to solve. A visual aid is just that—an *aid* to understanding, not a source of confusion. *Color* can promote clarity. Use colors to show different paths in a flow or system diagram or to identify different parts in an assembly or curves in a graph. Always give each visual a prominent *title* that captures the essence of the visual's message. *Label* every important part of the visual, but only the parts that are necessary to understanding. Do whatever you can to help the audience get the point quickly and without a lot of head scratching.

Remember, the *quality* of your visuals conveys a message. If they are scratched, contain sloppy lettering or amateurish clumsy artwork, or are obviously scrounged up from some other presentation, the visuals convey an impression much like that of wearing running shoes with a tuxedo.

Quality often reflects the degree of formality of a presentation—the more formal, the better the quality. The budget and the time available must also influence quality. Whatever the situation and the restraints, the quality of your visuals should be the best you can manage.

What resources are available to you? Even small companies usually have the means for producing basic artwork, 35-mm slides, and overhead transparencies. The larger the company, the more likely it is that a group, section, or department exists to provide professional assistance with visual design and production. If your organization does not have such a group, check into audiovisual services available from local firms.

Time—not money—is too often the factor that limits quality. It takes time to prepare artwork, just as it takes time to produce high-quality audiovisual materials. Plan your schedule to allow enough time for quality. All the money in the world cannot buy back time.

Visuals should be *appropriate* to the subject, the audience, and the situation. Be especially careful of cartoons and other humorous visuals. As with the audio channel, avoid humor that exploits, that is self-deprecating, or that may offend.

### Types of Visuals

From general rules, we next discuss the specific types of visuals used in business and technical presentations.

The most common problem encountered in the use of *word visuals* is simply using too many words. *Never* use complete sentences. The visual should show the fewest number of words that capture the ideas you wish to communicate. The two slides shown in Figure 7 illustrate this point. Both slides must be read by the audience, but the first one (A) is like a report. The speaker cannot add anything to the message. With slide B, the speaker provides the supporting detail. Slide B serves two functions: it highlights the speaker's message for the audience, and it becomes a cue card for the speaker.

Word slides should have no more than five to seven words per line (or forty characters) and no more than eight lines. Use bullets (●) or hyphens to emphasize key points. If the artwork for the visual is being

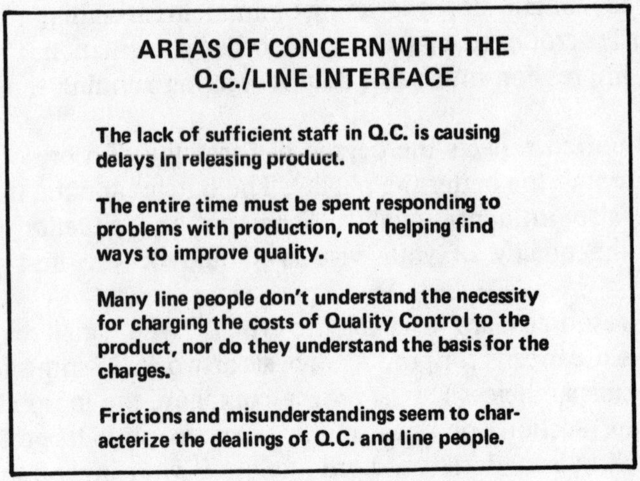

**AREAS OF CONCERN WITH THE
Q.C./LINE INTERFACE**

The lack of sufficient staff in Q.C. is causing delays in releasing product.

The entire time must be spent responding to problems with production, not helping find ways to improve quality.

Many line people don't understand the necessity for charging the costs of Quality Control to the product, nor do they understand the basis for the charges.

Frictions and misunderstandings seem to characterize the dealings of Q.C. and line people.

**Figure 7A** Too Wordy

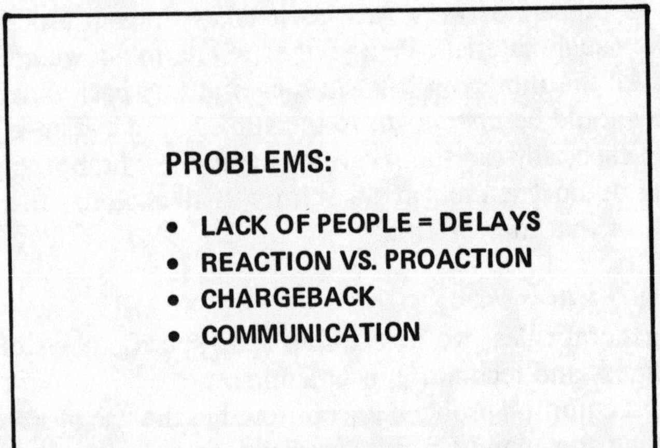

**PROBLEMS:**

- **LACK OF PEOPLE = DELAYS**
- **REACTION VS. PROACTION**
- **CHARGEBACK**
- **COMMUNICATION**

**Figure 7B** Key Words Only

typed, the 8½-by-11 inch sheets of paper should be inserted horizontally. The projection format for both 35-mm and overhead transparencies is wider than it is tall.

*Tables* are probably the most abused form of visual; they are also the most commonly used in business presentations. Tables compare statistical information, usually columns of figures, and most often each column represents a particular time. A presentation consisting of an unbroken series of tables is difficult enough for the audience, but if the tables themselves are difficult to interpret, the result is disastrous. Here are some suggestions for making tables easy to read and understand:

- Be ruthless with numbers; use the fewest possible numbers that will still convey the point of the visual. Try not to exceed twenty numbers.
- Combine numbers into larger sums wherever possible; eliminate any number that does not contribute significantly to the message of the visual.
- Do not use one huge table when you can split the data into two or three smaller tables. Remember—use no more than five or six columns per visual.
- Have a title that states the point of the visual. Put it at the top. Include a date below the table.
- Label the columns clearly at the top of each column. Show the units (dollars or tons, for example). On the left, label the statistics being compared.
- Avoid footnotes.
- Use light horizontal lines if they will improve readability.
- Be consistent. Do not mix pounds and tons, years and months, gross and net.
- Align decimal points vertically.
- Highlight the most important numbers with boxes, underlining, or with color.
- If arithmetic operations are not obvious, state them: (less), or "Less Depreciation Expense."
- Eliminate zeros by expressing numbers in thousands or millions, if possible.
- Show negative numbers in parentheses, not with minus signs.
- Finally, before producing the table, ask if the same information can be shown with a graph.

For an illustration of these points, study Table 4. Try to remember all the things that puzzle you—all the unanswered questions posed by the table. Now examine Table 5, which deals with the same subject, but presents it more clearly and more suitably for a visual. Now look at both

**Table 4** First Draft Prepared with a Typewriter

COST ESTIMATE

New Plastics Plant

| End of | 1/2 year 170,000 lb 73¢ lb | 1 year 454,000 lb 73¢ lb | 1-1/2 years 1,000,000 lb/yr 73¢ lb | 2 years 1,500,000 lb/yr 73¢ lb | 2-1/2 years 2,000,000 lb/yr 70¢ lb | 3 years 3,000,000 lb/yr 68¢ lb |
|---|---|---|---|---|---|---|
| Annual Sales Rate | $123,000 | $358,000 | $730,000 | $1,095,000 | $1,400,000 | $2,040,000 |
| Material | 77,000(45¢ lb) | 182,000(40¢ lb) | 400,000 | 600,000 | 800,000 | 1,200,000 |
| Labor | 27,000 | 47,000 | 100,000 | 150,000 | 200,000 | 300,000 |
| GROSS PROFIT | 19,000 | 129,000 | 230,000 | 345,000 | 400,000 | 540,000 |
| Factory Overhead | 82,500 | 82,500 | 82,500 | 82,500 | 100,000 | 100,000 |
| R & D | 12,000 | 12,000 | 20,000 | 30,000 | 35,000 | 40,000 |
| Administration | 51,000 | 51,000 | 51,000 | 51,000 | 55,000 | 60,000 |
| Sales | 30,500 | 30,500 | 35,500 | 40,000 | 40,000 | 50,000 |
| Total | 280,000 | 405,000 | 689,000 | 953,500 | 1,230,000 | 1,750,000 |
| Net Cash Flow | -157,000 | - 47,000 | 41,000 | 141,500 | 170,000 | 290,000 |
| Depreciation | 33,000 | 36,000 | 40,000 | 50,000 | 60,000 | 75,000 |
| Total Loss | -$190,000 | -$ 83,000 | +$ 1,000 | +$ 91,500 | +$ 110,000 | +$ 215,000 |

**Table 5** Final Typeset Draft

## 3-YEAR PROFIT PROJECTION:  NEW PLASTICS PLANT

|  | YEAR 1 | YEAR 2 | YEAR 3 |
|---|---|---|---|
| UNIT STATISTICS |  |  |  |
|    ANNUAL PRODUCTION RATE(000) | 454 | 1500 | 3000 |
|    PRICE PER POUND ($) | .73 | .73 | .68 |
|  |  |  |  |
| PROFIT & LOSS SUMMARY |  |  |  |
| (ALL FIGURES ARE ANNUALIZED) |  |  |  |
|  |  |  |  |
| PROJECTED SALES ($000) | 358 | 1095 | 2040 |
|   COST OF SALES |  |  |  |
|     MATERIAL | 182 | 600 | 1200 |
|     LABOR | 47 | 150 | 300 |
|   OTHER COSTS |  |  |  |
|     OVERHEAD | 82.5 | 82.5 | 100 |
|     ENGINEERING | 12 | 30 | 40 |
|     ADMINISTRATION | 51 | 51 | 60 |
|     SALES EXPENSE | 30.5 | 40 | 50 |
| TOTAL COST | 405 | 953.5 | 1750 |
| PROFIT CONTRIBUTION | (47) | 141.5 | 290 |
| LESS DEPRECIATION | 36 | 50 | 75 |
| PROFIT BEFORE TAX | (83) | 91.5 | 215 |

tables. Compare the titles, the headings, the level of detail, and finally, the differences in typography. Table 4 was produced with a standard typewriter. Table 5 was produced on composition equipment. Even though Table 5 may not be the ideal way to present the information, it is an enormous improvement over the original version.

*Graphs* are useful for showing trends or comparisons. They provide information at a glance without giving stacks of specific numbers, as tables do. Graphs of any kind are used for visualizing numerical information. Whenever it is not necessary to show actual numbers, use graphs.

*Bar graphs* are especially useful for comparing separate quantities, and also work well at showing trends. The bars shown in Figure 8 illustrate that both positive and negative values may be shown (A and B). Notice that when the bars are segmented, as in C and D, it is

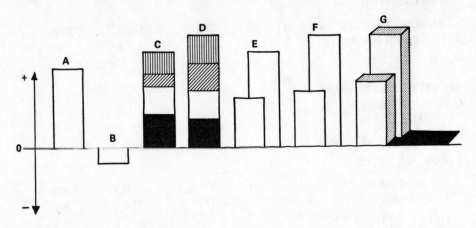

**Figure 8** Typical Bar Graphs

difficult to see the differences in the top three segments, because they lack a common base line. Bars E and F solve the problem by using the same base line. Graphic artists have many techniques for adding impact to bar graphs. Bar G shows just a hint of the possibilities. Bar graphs are meant to simplify the showing of numerical information. Do not throw away that advantage by putting all the numbers back in (see Figure 9). Bar graphs can also be used to show the proportionate parts of a whole (see Figure 10).

*Circle graphs* or pie charts are often used for the same purpose. They work best when the wedges of the pie are all more than 3 percent and the number of wedges does not exceed eight. A problem with circle graphs is that people have difficulty perceiving angular differences. A sector can be twice the size of its neighbor and we may fail to realize it. Do not burden the visual by adding both the quantities and the percentages to the pieces of pie.

*Line graphs* are the mainstay of many technical presentations. They show the relationship between interacting phenomena as well as trends over time. Sadly, many scientists, engineers, and technical specialists

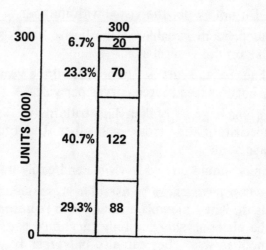

**Figure 9** Too Many Numbers

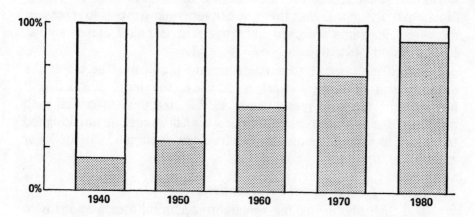

**Figure 10** Bar Graph Showing Proportions

use the same graph they plotted in the lab as artwork for a visual. The result is catastrophic! The lettering is too small. The curves are too thin and too numerous. The entire visual is dominated (even blackened) by the grid lines of the graph paper.

Here are a few suggestions for making good visuals with line graphs:

- Use the smallest possible number of grid lines. Use tick marks in place of grid lines wherever possible.
- Do not include footnotes, explanations, or other secondary data in

the visual. Do not clutter the visual with numbers.

- Plot the independent variable on the horizontal axis, the dependent variable on the vertical axis.
- Use thick lines for the curves. Do not crowd the visual with many curves; try not to exceed three curves per visual.
- Use colors, shading, or broken line patterns to distinguish the curves, especially if they cross each other. Use broken lines to show extrapolation.
- The grid units should be highly visible and easily understood.

*Diagrams and schematics* can be useful in presentations. A *diagram* is a line drawing designed to explain rather than represent something. Diagrams can be pictorial, showing only functional parts of a device, usually in a simplified way. They can also be verbal. In the block diagram, activities, operations, or parts of systems, are represented by words inside rectangles or other shapes. *Schematics* show all of the functional parts of a device; they use conventional symbols to represent the parts. Diagrams are used extensively in technical presentations; schematics only occasionally (see Figure 11).

Both diagrams and schematics present problems. The closer the diagram gets to being a *working* drawing, the more unsuitable it becomes for use in a presentation. PERT diagrams, or critical path diagrams, decision trees, and piping or wiring diagrams are not designed to be used as visuals; neither are electronic or pneumatic schematics or mechanical drawings.

### Visuals for Technical Presentations

The challenge in making visuals for technical presentations is to provide a level of detail that will help the audience focus on your message and prevent them from spending their time exploring the wonderful intricacies and details they see before them. All of the characteristics of effective visuals apply to technical presentations. The problem is that these characteristics are usually harder to achieve, especially *simplicity, readability, and clarity.* Here are some ideas for creating effective visuals for technical presentations.

- Do not use working documents for visuals.
- Use simple diagrams to give an overview of your subject, then explain the details one by one with *separate* visuals. Do not talk for more than two minutes with any visual.

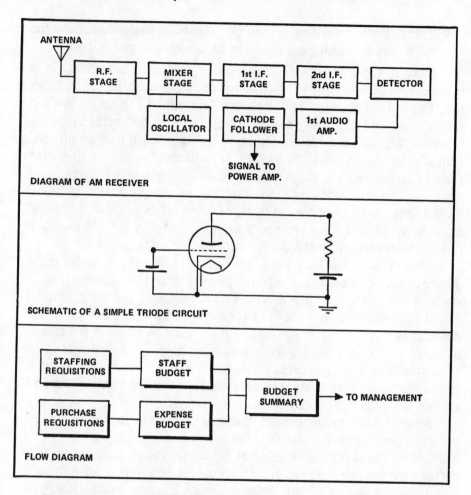

**Figure 11** Diagrams and Schematics

- If you must show a large, complex diagram, do it in stages. With an overhead projector, you can cover the visual with a sheet of paper and uncover parts of the diagram as needed. Of course, this technique works only if the diagram lends itself to being explained area by area. If systems overlap, use overlays (one or more slides on top of the first) to build the diagram in stages. With 35-mm slides, the diagram can be photographed as each stage is added, thus producing the same gradual buildup.

- Schematics should be used only if every member of your audience is familiar with the symbols.

● Always keep the audience in mind. What can be done to make the visual simple, clear, and readable to this particular audience?

*Pictures* (35-mm slides) add interest, color, and realism. In a technical presentation, they are fine for showing what the object looks like, but not for showing how it works. Photographs usually show too much detail and too many nonfunctional parts to be useful by themselves in technical exposition. (Imagine trying to learn how an internal combustion engine works by looking at pictures of engines and engine parts.) Use diagrams to explain function in tandem with photographs to show appearance, size, location. For expository purposes, technical illustrations have two big advantages over photographs. Technical illustrations do not show unimportant detail and they can cut away the outside to reveal and highlight the functioning parts within.

*Models and mockups* may be useful adjuncts to a technical presentation. A model is a replica of some object or device, usually made to scale. It may or may not operate. One reason for using a model is that the real object will not fit in (or cannot be brought to) the room. Another is that the real object does not yet exist. A mockup is a replica of some part of an object, usually much simplified and designed to show function. The classical example is the wooden representation of a piston, connecting rod, crankshaft, cylinder walls, and valves used to explain the principle of internal combustion.

Models and mockups are unusual in business and technical presentations largely because they are expensive. The expense has to be justified by the stakes (as with an architectural model for a new building), or by the fact that the presentation will be given repeatedly to a very large number of people. Another limiting factor is that the size of the model or mockup usually limits its use to small audiences. This limitation can be overcome in part, however, by using 35-mm slides of the model from every important viewing angle.

### Recognizing Effective Visuals

Reading this section has not made you an expert in designing professional visuals, but it has covered the range of visuals available to you. It also has helped you to recognize what makes a visual effective. The qualities of effective visuals are:

| | |
|---|---|
| Unity | Readability |
| Simplicity | Clarity |
| Economy | Quality |
| Consistency | Appropriateness |

Planning and designing visuals are skills that one learns by doing. Each frame presents a different challenge. No two solutions are alike, and each new solution produces new learning. To help quicken your learning, seek the advice and assistance of the specialists in your organization or even of an audiovisual design firm if the stakes are high enough to justify the expense.

## THE IMPORTANCE OF BALANCE

The most common flaw in script preparation for a presentation is a lack of balance between the audio and the visual channels. The special power of the audiovisual presentation derives in part from its two-channel approach to communication. Both channels should contribute equally to the work. Here is a list of common problems that can occur in trying to balance the two channels.

### Overloading

This occurs when the visual is so complex or so packed with information that the audience cannot cope with both channels simultaneously. When you use such a visual, you, in effect, are saying to your audience, "You must choose between listening to me or absorbing what you are seeing." The audience will nearly always choose the visual channel because it is more arresting. Your voice, to which they have grown accustomed, will fade into the background.

How do you prevent overloading? First, avoid cramming too much information into one visual. Break the material into several manageable visuals. Next, if a complex visual must be used, show it in stages by uncovering and discussing it in stages. In that way you can gradually guide your audience through the complexities. Finally, if you *must* show a visual that will cause overloading, stop talking; give your audience time to process the information. In such a case, the audio portion of the script might read as follows: "This table shows the managerial, professional, clerical and production staffing we will encounter in the next twenty-four months." (Pause) Simply wait for your audience to absorb the material before continuing.

### Weak Visual Channel

Have you ever listened to a person speak for five minutes while displaying only a one-word visual? Next time it happens, watch the audience. Those who are paying attention will either be looking at the speaker or restlessly glancing at both the speaker and the screen. Those who are elsewhere mentally will be gazing at that single word as if it had hypnotic power!

We seldom see one-word visuals, but a similar practice, using the visual channel for merely showing *topics,* is all too common. Usually the speaker fills in the supporting detail by dull readings from notes. If the *subtopics* were included in the visual, however, the speaker would not need notes or cue cards (the cues would be in the visual), and the audience would have a more interesting, useful visual channel.

### Failure to Integrate the Two Channels

Each channel should provide information. If the speaker is simply reading the visuals to the audience, the audio channel adds nothing. In fact, the speaker is unnecessary. The audience can read without anyone's help. Balance in a script means that the channels complement each other. Each channel should do some of the work. Balance also means that the content of the sounds and images is closely related, working in harmony to accomplish the mission of each frame. In short, don't show one thing and talk about something else.

## SUMMARY

Preparing a script is an exercise in making choices. You must choose the most suitable *words* to convey your message in the audio channel. You must choose the *visual medium* (or combination of media) that will best satisfy the requirements of your presentation. Then, you must choose, frame by frame, the *type of visual* that best supports, illustrates, amplifies, or reinforces the information in the audio channel. Choose wisely and well! After the choices are made, your completed script serves as a blueprint for the design of the visuals. Once the visuals are produced, you are almost ready to deliver the presentation.

# 7
# Step Six: Consider the Physical Factors

One common mistake speakers make is ignoring the purely physical elements of a presentation. Yet it is almost impossible to communicate with another human being without satisfying at least a threshold of physical comfort. For example, an audience cannot concentrate its attention for long periods unless the room temperature is within a narrow band (about 68 to 75 degrees F.). The presentation *itself*, after all, is a purely physical act.

The objective of this chapter is to help you become sensitive to the physical aspects of audience communication so that you will avoid distractions and heighten your audience's ability to absorb your message. We begin with the environment.

## THE ROOM

If you can exercise control over the presentation room, by all means do so. Here is a checklist to help you choose a room suitable for your presentation.

*The temperature* is most critical, as mentioned. Rooms that are too hot are to be avoided at all costs. People usually can get warm by putting on more clothing, but social norms severely limit the extent to which one may disrobe in public. Few things can annoy, distract, and stupefy an audience more than a warm, humid room. Remember that each member of your audience will generate heat when the room is full. Find a cool room.

*The size* is important, too. Rooms that are too small can create severe discomfort for people who need a large bubble of space around them to be comfortable. Rooms that are vastly oversized for the audience can create an eerie, vault-like effect.

*The shape* of a room influences both a speaker's ability to make contact with the members of the audience and their ability to see, hear, 77 and communicate with each other. Generally, it is wise to avoid long, narrow rooms; they usually require you to overpower the people in front in order to reach those at the rear of the room. Moreover, people must lean and crane their necks to see you and the screen. Long, narrow rooms can inhibit discussion between audience members. I prefer rooms that are square, or nearly so. They allow the audience to see and hear more easily and the speaker to move about more freely.

*The acoustics* should be adequate. If the room is acoustically too absorbent (heavy drapes, thick rugs, acoustic ceilings, and/or padded furniture), your voice will be soaked up like water pouring over dry sand. You will have to shout to be heard by everyone. At the opposite extreme is the room that is so acoustically bright or reflective that the reverberations bouncing off hard walls actually compete with the direct sound of your voice. Is the room so large or the acoustics so poor that you will need to use a public address system?

*Microphones* should be considered. If you need a PA system, avoid fixed microphones. Using them requires a good deal of skill. You must keep your mouth constantly at the same distance from a fixed mike, or the volume will fade. This restricts head and body movements. In effect, you become a prisoner of the microphone. Use a *lapel* mike (clips to your blouse, tie, or lapel), or a *lavalier* mike (hangs from your neck), or a *wireless* mike, which allows you to move about without worrying about a microphone cord. Whatever kind you use, make sure the volume and tone controls are set correctly for your voice before the presentation.

*Air circulation* is vital in a presentation room. Without adequate circulation, your audience will be annoyed by cigarette, pipe, and cigar smoke, or simply their own stale air.

*Darkening capability* is important if you intend to show 35-mm slides or movies. The best rooms can be partially darkened with dimmers to allow audience members to take notes.

*The arrangement* of the chairs and the speaker's space is especially important. Try to place the speaker so that there are no distractions behind him (such as doors or windows) or near him. An instance involving a poor arrangement occurred recently when a company invited a college professor, who was a renowned expert in his field, to lecture to a group of its employees. The speaker was flown 2,000 miles to speak in a hall that looked like the one shown in Figure 12. The professor began the talk at 1:30 P.M. A seemingly endless procession of latecomers was forced to walk directly in front of the speaker to enter

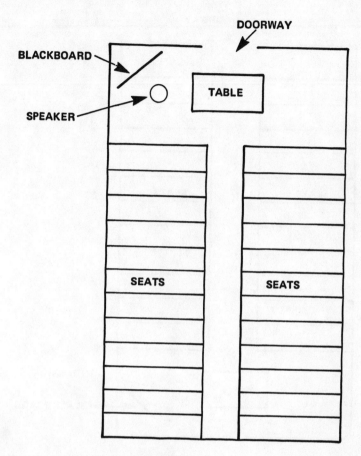

**Figure 12** Speaker Near the Doorway

the room. After ten minutes of constant interruption, the professor ran out of funny lines. The last straggler sheepishly entered the room at 3:00 P.M.—an hour and a half later. The occasion was a monumental disaster! If someone had thought about the physical arrangement of the room, the results could have been quite different (see Figure 13). With this arrangement, the inevitable latecomers could have taken their seats without distracting either the professor or the audience.

### Arranging the Seats and Visuals

Give careful attention to the seating and screen placement. Most importantly, be sure everyone in the room can see the visuals. Figure 14 suggests four of many acceptable arrangements.

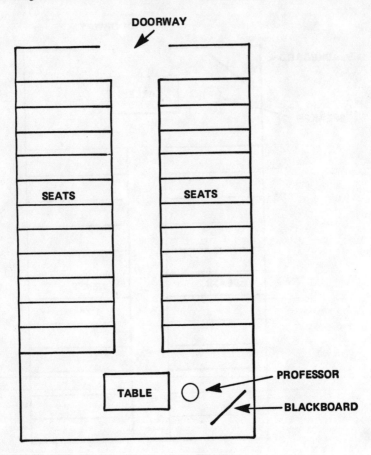

**Figure 13** Speaker Opposite the Doorway

The overhead projector works best with the screen set at an angle to the audience. The image can be viewed clearly at fairly steep angles, as much as thirty degrees from the plane of the screen. Use a beaded screen for the widest viewing angle.

If the screen in the meeting room is permanently fixed and parallel to the audience (as is most often the case), you have a problem with the overhead projector. Your body, and perhaps the projector itself, will block the view of several people. Before the audience arrives, move the chairs that give an obstructed view of the screen.

The 35-mm projector can be used with the screen parallel to the audience, as shown in C and D (Figure 14), or it can be used at an angle. Be sure to *raise* the 35-mm projector high enough to project over

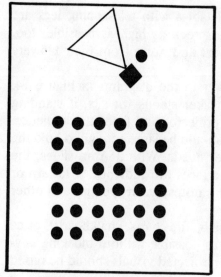

**A. AUDITORIUM STYLE WITH OVERHEAD PROJECTOR**

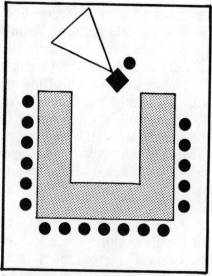

**B. CONFERENCE STYLE WITH OVERHEAD PROJECTOR**

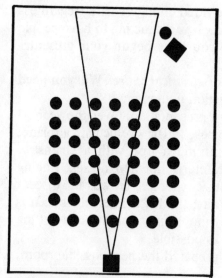

**C. AUDITORIUM STYLE WITH 35mm PROJECTOR**

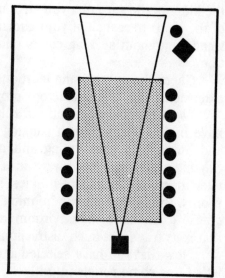

**D. CONFERENCE STYLE WITH 35mm PROJECTOR**

**Figure 14** Typical Room Arrangements

the heads of your audience. Special tables with telescoping legs are available for this purpose. Raise the screen as high as possible, too. Always place projectors where the heat and noise from their blowers will not annoy and distract anyone.

Notice the location of the speaker in the diagrams in Figure 14. With the overhead projector, the speaker stands (or sits, if standing blocks someone's view) beside the projector and faces the audience. The table on which the projector sits should be large enough to hold the visuals and whatever else the speaker needs. With 35-mm slides, the speaker stands next to the screen and faces the audience. A lectern or table is placed nearby for the speaker's notes, water, pointer and other needs.

For nonprojected media (easel pads, flip charts, chalkboard), place the visuals as close to the audience as possible without blocking anyone's view. For large groups, the nonprojected visuals should be raised so that the people sitting in back can see them.

The *chairs* should be comfortable. One maker of fold-up chairs has designed a hard metal chair that is best described as the acme of discomfort. The back of the chair slices audience members just above the kidneys. Be sure that you have provided enough chairs (regardless of the kind) to seat all of your audience. It is distracting to have people wandering about seeking chairs once you have begun your presentation.

Check the number and locations of *electrical outlets*. Will you need extension cords to operate your projection equipment?

*Distractions* of any kind can ruin a presentation. Over the years, I have had to compete with banging pipes, traffic (vehicular, airplane, and human), a man felling and trimming a tree with a chainsaw, clinking plates and silverware in a cafeteria, kitchen noises, ringing telephones, the sounds of movies, music, cheering crowds in adjacent rooms, the roar of air conditioning units; the list is interminable. It is crucial to examine the environment thoughtfully and select a setting that is as free from such distractions as possible.

Now that you have selected and prepared the best possible room, let's bring some people into it.

## WHAT TIME?

As with selecting a room, if you can choose the time of your presentation, by all means do so. Choose a time when your audience is most likely to be physically ready and mentally alert. I recently asked a group what was the worst day of the week to have a presentation. One wag responded, "Sunday!" Most people agree that in a *normal* work week, Monday mornings and Friday afternoons are less than ideal. Another time to avoid if possible is immediately after lunch (especially if lunch includes an alcoholic beverage). The body seems to respond to the problem of processing food more readily than processing ideas. Less serious, but still worth avoiding is an early morning or late afternoon presentation. Some of us are slow starters, and the ones who are not (the morning people) are likely to have lost that sharp edge by 4 P.M. Figure 15 is a chart of the ideal times to conduct presentations. Of course, one cannot always achieve perfection; but if you can choose the time, choose one that will enhance your chances of success.

## HOW LONG?

What is the limit of an audience's endurance? I must thank Professor Brian Quinn of Dartmouth College for introducing me to the term *Fanny Factor*. (The brain will absorb no more than the fanny will.) But there is also an attention-span factor, a lack-of-body-movement factor, a thirst factor, a hunger factor and, the most pressing of all, the bladder factor. These limitations of the human machine dictate an absolute endurance limit of about 1¼ to 1½ hours. Beyond that limit, the bodies may still be in the room, but many of the minds will begin to leave.

Audiences will tell you when they need a break. Look for the signs: facial expressions, posture, gestures (such as glancing at watches), shuffling feet, even a kind of dreamy lassitude can signal that it is time to stop and recharge batteries.

## THE EQUIPMENT

Of course you will not forget to have a projector in the room, but what other equipment will you need? Here is a checklist of other equipment and related items:

| | |
|---|---|
| Slides | Easel |
| Screen | Easel pad |
| Table for projector | Easel pad marker |
| Back-up projector | P.A. system |
| Spare projector bulb | Lectern |
| Spare fuses | Extension cords (electrical) |
| Blackboard | 3-Prong adapter |
| Chalk | Handouts |
| Eraser | Flip charts |
| Pointer (metal, wooden, or optical) | Masking tape (2-inches wide) |
| Grease pencil | Audiovisual assistant |

Extension cord for 35-mm-slide-advancing control

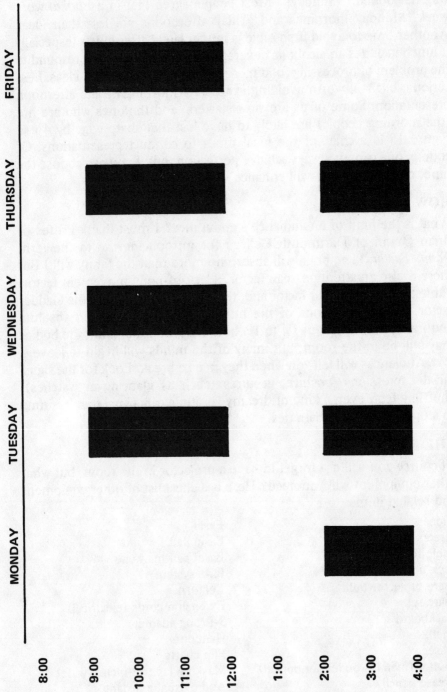

**Figure 15** Optimum Times for Presentations

You should always plan to arrive early. Make sure the projection equipment is set up, focussed, and operating properly. Go through all the visuals to ensure they are in correct order and none is positioned upside down or backwards. Then check to make sure that you and your audience will have everything you both will need.

## OTHER NECESSITIES

Here is a checklist of items not related to equipment but equally important (some are optional):

Chairs (arranged properly)
Tables (ditto)
Water for you
Water for them
Ashtrays
Nametags
Place cards
Writing pads

Pencils
A copy of the agenda
Coffee
Decaffeinated coffee
Tea
Soft drinks
Juice

One final piece of advice: When it comes to physical considerations, never take chances and never take anything for granted. Murphy's Law states: "Whatever can go wrong . . . will."

Murphy was an optimist.

# 8
# Step Seven: Deliver Your Presentation

We have arrived at the final plateau. All of the thinking, planning, organizing, writing, choosing, designing—all the preparation has led to this, the *physical act* of communicating with your audience.

Delivering a presentation requires that you use your body to convey information and ideas, that you use it so that the focus of the audience is centered on the message, not on you. But you cannot be merely a passive transmission device. Audiences view your material as an extension of *you*. They are just as interested in getting a sense of you as they are in hearing your message. Your goal as a presenter is not only to intensify your audience's awareness of your subject with a minimum of distractions, but to communicate a positive sense of *you* as well.

## WHAT IS SO DIFFICULT?

Speaking to an audience can have spooky effects on some people. Bright, warm, articulate men and women who are confident and outgoing in private conversations suddenly undergo complete personality changes when they speak to an audience. They become awed by an audience, shy, introverted, unnatural, awkward, and uncomfortable. They stare at the floor, hide their hands, or use them to clutch or fiddle with objects. They speak too quietly, too quickly, or too haltingly, or in voices devoid of vitality and animation. In short, they become strangers. Indeed, *The Book of Lists** reports that Americans rank "speaking before a group" as their number one fear. They evidently dread it more than death itself!

The purpose of this section is not to transform you into another Clarence Darrow or Demosthenes; the aim is simply to help you use

---

*David Wallechinsky, Irving Wallace, and Amy Wallace
86 (New York: Wm. Morrow, 1977).

the communication skills you acquired as a child along with the physical and mental equipment you possess as an adult in order to speak effectively and competently with audiences as *yourself,* without apprehension or unreasonable expectations.

## THE QUEST FOR PERFECTION

Probably the most unreasonable expectation is that you must be perfect. You must represent the highest form, the most advanced development of *homo sapiens.* Not one mispronounced word, not one imperfect gesture, not a cough or a stutter or a single "um" is permissible. If you seek perfection, you are programming yourself for failure.

Perhaps because most of the speakers we see on television seem perfect (most of the time), we have come to expect a standard of excellence far beyond what is realistic. Television performers are made up, have professional lighting and set designers, and most crucially, have teleprompters to tell them exactly what to say. The visual channel is operated by a team of professionals. To expect such perfection in everyday business or technical presentations is not only unrealistic, it is also positively destructive.

Trying to be perfect will cause you to use elaborate notes, for example, so that every word will be precise and not even a subtle point will be omitted. (You will probably end up awkwardly reading notes to your audience.) Trying to be perfect can cause you to seem ill at ease or uncomfortable or simply to give the impression that you are trying too hard.

Audiences are far less sensitive to our imperfections than we are ourselves. Most audiences tend to ignore or accept them unless they become distracting. In fact, an occasional slip can reassure them that you, too, are human!

## TRYING TO BE SOMEBODY ELSE

In group critiques, I often hear comments like this: "I have known John for ten years and somehow he seemed different during his presentation. His voice was different. He did things with his hands I have never seen him do before. He just wasn't John." Early in life, we seem to acquire the tendency to be somebody else when giving a presentation. Have you ever seen a child recite a poem in a stilted recitation voice, standing with legs crossed, eyes fixed on the ceiling, an apprehensive look on the face, hands clasped behind the back with the whole body rocking back and forth? Then shortly after the applause, little Martha suddenly becomes a real child again, her natural behavior in striking contrast to that of her recitation person.

The most frequent advice given to people seeking to improve their public speaking is *be yourself*. This is good advice, but like the tips "don't worry" or "relax" it is sometimes hard to follow. Here are a few thoughts that can help give you the confidence to be yourself.

One of my clients once said that in delivering an extremely important presentation he put on the best "Orson Welles imitation" he could muster. I quickly informed him of the error of his ways. Imitating another speaker's style is not a good idea. The best one can hope for is a second-rate Orson Welles or Winston Churchill. What is needed is a first rate *you*. The audience wants to get a sense of who *you* are, of what *your* style is like.

Try to forget the notions that you have to be special when you speak before a group of people, or that you must impress your audience. This frame of mind will produce your recitation person, not the real you.

## RULES OF DELIVERY

### Rule One: Engagement

*Question:* If you could reduce delivery skill to one word, what would that word be?

*Answer:* Delivery skill cannot be reduced to one word, but the word that comes closest is *engagement. Engagement* means reaching out to make contact with your audience. It means coming forward and meeting the audience on its own terms. If you engage an audience, they know it; it shows in your voice, your face, your movements.

### Rule Two: Energy

Listening is hard work, requiring a huge amount of total energy on the part of an audience. A skillful speaker must work as hard at delivering as the audience does at listening. This means that you must give up *energy*. The energy flows outward from your voice, face, eyes— from your entire body. If the speaker's energy level is low, the whole delivery takes on a low-key, lackluster quality. The voice is soft and without animation. The face and eyes lack vitality and expression. The body seems passive. Energy means vitality and dynamism, and you must provide it. *You* are the engine that makes a presentation go.

## Rule Three: Empathy

Earlier in this book we discussed analyzing your audience. Once you have the profile of your audience, it should influence every step that follows. Delivery is no exception.

A skilled presenter is *audience-centered*, not *self-centered*. Empathy is the ability to *become* your audience, to imagine what it is like to be sitting out there experiencing your presentation. Audiences sense when a speaker is involved with them, and they respond to it. By focussing your attention on the audience you will create a rapport with them. You will also avoid the pitfalls that accompany self-centeredness. You will be asking mental questions such as:

Can that woman in the back row hear me?

Does he follow me?

Are they getting tired?

Do they need a break?

Can this person up front see the visual?

Is the pace too fast?

Does he have a question?

You will *not* be asking mental questions such as:

Do they like me?

Am I doing well?

Do they sense how nervous I am?

Is my tie straight?

Can they see the stain on my jacket?

Do they know I'm nervous?

The presenter who has empathy is constantly looking and listening for audience feedback. Facial expressions, movements, gestures, sounds, eye contact, posture—all are messages. If you are in tune with your audience, you will be sensitive to these nonverbal cues and respond to them by changing your pace, asking a question, stopping for a break, or doing whatever seems appropriate.

## Impact on Delivery

Engagement, energy, and empathy are all interlocking elements in the process of audience communication. When one or more of these elements is missing, the impact on delivery is predictable; the speaker displays:

- Little or no eye contact
- A voice that lacks volume and dynamics
- Awkward posture
- Lack of movement (or perpetual motion)
- Distracting mannerisms
- Absence of pauses
- Improper vocal pace
- Ill-at-ease, uncomfortable manner (or overdone performance)
- Inability to establish rapport with audience

The physical act of delivering a presentation requires that you use your voice and your body to communicate and interact with an audience. Let us examine how engagement, energy, and empathy can influence the dynamics of speech and the attitudes and actions of the body to enhance communication.

## THE VOICE

In an audiovisual presentation, the voice is the audio channel, carrying half of the message. Thus, half of the task of making contact with the audience depends on what you do with your vocal chords. What you do with your voice can mean the difference between an audience that is working to listen or is simply loafing. What are the characteristics that make a voice *listenable?*

### Volume

Most people speak too softly to audiences. Clearly you cannot conduct an effective presentation if no one can hear you. The usual solution is to advise people to "speak up" or "project your voice to the back of the room." Good advice, but let's go beyond merely speaking louder.

We can divide our vocal and physical presence into zones of communication. The smallest is the *intimate zone.* In the intimate zone, two people are bending close to each other and whispering. The intent is to contain the sounds and restrict them to the participants. Little or no body movement is used beyond cupping the hand over the listener's ear. In the *personal zone* (about four to six feet), we converse with little attempt to project the voice and we use small movements of the head and hands. In the *social zone* (six to twelve feet), we begin to project our voice outward and to use the body—especially the head and hands—to emphasize our words. A party with six or eight people standing in a circle is a good example of communicating in our social zone. In the *group zone* (twelve to forty feet or so), we are speaking to audiences. Here, we must raise the volume of the voice to fill the room. This requires constant effort and may seem unnatural to those unaccustomed to speaking in this zone. It is, nonetheless, utterly necessary. The body movements are more pronounced as well.

Experienced speakers develop a sense of the size of the acoustic space they are in and they fill that space with their voice. They also tailor their body movements to the space—the larger the space, the more pronounced the movement. The level of volume and the presence that are correct for a group of fifteen in a small room are not correct for a group of fifty people in a large hall.

A final bit of advice: if you must err with your volume level, let it be on the side of too much volume, not too little. (Remember rule number two: energy.)

### Vocal Pace

Have you ever had to listen to a speaker who talked too fast or too slowly? If so, you may recall how frustrating it was not to be able to control the pace. You may also recall how easy and tempting it was to focus your eyes on the middle distance and slip away mentally. Now change roles. You are the speaker. You control the vocal pace. It is up to you to choose the rate at which your audience will hear your words. How do you choose? Here are some guidelines for deciding at what pace to speak.

### *Do Not Rush*

An audience can process words for short periods at over 800 per minute, but you cannot possibly talk that fast and you shouldn't try. A too-rapid delivery strips the voice of all the elements of listenability for the sake of speed. The voice tends to become flat and mechanical; pauses are rare. The faster the pace, the more difficult it becomes to speak distinctly. The audience (despite its 800-plus word processing capacity) eventually grows tired of the struggle and drops out. The ideal pace is quick enough to hold the audience's attention without inducing fatigue.

### Do Not Dawdle

If the vocal pace is too slow, the audience will have too much free time. Audience members often will use the extra time to think about subjects unrelated to yours but of immediate and compelling interest to them. Eventually, those preoccupations begin to command most of their attention. Sooner or later members return from their ruminations (or their reveries) to your words only to discover that in their absence they missed something important. Then, faced with the double problem of not understanding a speaker whose delivery is ponderously slow; they return for good to their private worlds of thought . . . and your voice . . . fades into oblivion. . . .

### Vary the Pace

Wouldn't it be convenient if some expert discovered that the ideal vocal pace is exactly 148 words per minute? We could practice with a tape recorder until we spoke automatically at the perfect rate, and never be concerned about pace again. Unfortunately, there is no single ideal pace. An audience is composed of people who react individually to your voice. An ideal pace for one person may seem a bit fast for someone in the next seat. Speaking at one pace also would be boring. Try to imagine how difficult it would be to listen to someone speaking at the same unvarying rate for one hour. Audiences expect changes of pace; this is part of what makes vocal delivery interesting.

Even more important is the relationship between *idea density* and vocal pace. It makes sense to speak more slowly when explaining complex material or stressing an important point. It is equally sensible to quicken the pace when covering material that the audience can easily absorb.

### Use Feedback

Look and listen for the messages from your audience. Confused expressions, gestures of helplessness, and vacant stares usually mean that you are speaking too fast. Slouching, glances at wristwatches, doodling, and more vacant stares can signal that you should pick up the pace. The ideal pace is constantly varying to suit *this* audience, *this* information, and the needs of *this* moment in the course of the presentation.

## *Pauses*

Closely related to vocal pace is the subject of how to use pauses in delivery. Most beginning speakers fail to pause at all (beyond the natural stops to inhale). This is usually due to nervousness and a lack of empathy—to an inward rather than an outward focus. Accomplished speakers, in contrast, use pauses deliberately and effectively. Pauses not only make the voice more listenable, but they also have useful roles to play in delivery. Three types of pauses are:

- *Anticipation*—The speaker builds to a climactic point then pauses, holding the audience in suspense, before delivering the climax.

  Example: "I realize that if we approve this measure, only 1 person in 200,000 will contract cancer, but do you know who that person is? (Pause . . .) It is *you!*" (A bit melodramatic, but you see the point.)

- *Reinforcement*—This pause comes *after* you have made a telling point or explained a key relationship; the pause reinforces the point. First, your pause indicates that the point is important. Second, the pause gives the audience time to let the point register.

- *Rest*—Besides providing emphasis in the two ways mentioned, pauses can also provide relief. Listening, as you know, is hard work. An occasional pause merely for brief relaxation is a welcome change.

It is easy to misuse pauses. For example, constantly stopping in the middle of thoughts will distract an audience. In fact, any repetitive pattern will eventually become annoying. Too many pauses will create the impression that you are constantly collecting your thoughts. Very long pauses at inappropriate times make you seem lost.

Pauses are essential to listenability; without them, a voice becomes uninteresting. One thing that makes music interesting is silence—or rather, the patterns of sounds and silences. This pattern is even more vital in speeches, where the sounds carry information.

## *Animation*

The word comes from the Latin *animare:* to quicken, enliven, or endow with breath or soul. When applied to speech, animation is the quality that enlivens the voice, that gives it vitality and interest. The animation in your voice tells the audience how you feel about your words. Take any simple word, such as "yes." Now say "yes" in response to the following questions:

Is this your wallet, Mister?

Haven't I warned you a thousand times that this would happen?

Don't you think it's high time you gave him a piece of your mind?

Do you really love me, Harold?

The differences you hear in your voice are the result of *animation*. Animation also contributes to the meaning of our statements: "Charles, the way you handle a car is *incredible.*" How you say that last word has a lot to do with Charles's reaction.

Without animation, the voice becomes lifeless and uninteresting. In films, robots are almost always given flat mechanical voices. They are expected to sound lifeless. A human voice without animation is described as a monotone, and it is just as deadening. Few things short of knock-out drops can induce sleep more quickly than a monotone.

Of course, it is possible to carry animation to extremes. Occasionally (but rarely) a speaker's animation is so exaggerated and bubbly that it seems contrived and unnatural. By far the more common problem, however, is little or no animation at all.

Your voice should carry your convictions, concerns, and feelings by the way you stress certain syllables, the inflections, and the changes in pitch and intensity.

### Vocal Noise

Vocal noise is verbal garbage that litters and clutters our speech. Some of the most common nonsense words include: *You know, I mean, Like, Uh, Um, Ah, OK* (also *OK?*), *Right,* and *And.* It is possible to utter entire sentences consisting only of vocal noise:

I mean like Ah you know what I mean, right?

Vocal noise is distracting. If you use *any* expression frequently enough, your audience will notice it. Eventually they will concentrate on the noise and not the message.

Vocal noise is our way of filling in the gaps in speech. Our brain needs time to encode the next message. While our brain is working to turn thoughts into words, our vocal chords are stalling for time. We keep our vocal motor running: 1) to let the audience know that the next message is on the way; 2) to keep from being interrupted, and 3) to fill the time with words, even if they are sterile, useless words.

Vocal noise can be eradicated in two ways: First, you must *hear yourself* while you speak. Example:

(I mean) if you listen to (you know) your own voice (you know), (like) eventually you (Ah) will (you know) begin to (like) hear the garbage.

Admittedly this example is a caricature, but the point is valid. Listen to your words. You cannot stop making the noise until you detect it!

Second, you must be both confident and comfortable enough to let silences occur where you now use noise. Vocal noise is the enemy of the pause, and in this struggle, you must be on the side of the pause.

### Articulation

Audiences can react to how you pronounce words. For example, have you ever heard these words: Gonna, Coulda, Wooda, Din't, Effit, Tenative, Twenny, Deeze? Sure, we hear them all the time. We scarcely notice any but the most flagrant cases of sloppy speech *in conversation*.

But we *do* notice poor enunciation in a speaker. The rules change. Not that audiences expect perfection; they don't. In fact, if you were to articulate every sound perfectly, your voice would sound artificial, contrived, unnatural and would itself become a distraction. But we do tend to make judgments (almost always incorrect) about a speaker's intelligence or competence if we hear many words pronounced sloppily or incorrectly.

It is a good idea to speak distinctly when talking to an audience, not merely to avoid sending false messages about your intelligence but also to ensure that your words are easily understood.

Nervousness often causes us to speak too quickly. Of course, the more quickly we speak, the more difficult it becomes to articulate our words. Frequently the simple advice, "Slow down and speak carefully" works wonders with a nervous speaker. A more serious problem occurs when we have built-in articulation difficulties; that is, when we say certain words carelessly under any circumstances.

The first step in correcting poor articulation is the same for correcting vocal noise: you must *hear yourself*. Once you recognize the little flaws in your speech, you can work to eliminate them. A tape recorder can be very helpful in this process. Try reading naturally into a tape recorder. Be sure to read a long passage (at least five minutes) to ensure that you have dropped your tape recorder voice. An even better method is to record your voice in a real speech. When you play the tape listen carefully to how you pronounce the words. Listen for missing *t*'s, *d*'s, *-ing*'s, or the substituting of a single sound for a whole word, such as *shouda* for *should have.*

Listen for lapses into mumbling. Sometimes we end our sentences by trailing off. The volume drops and the pace quickens, as if the speaker wishes to get the sentence over and go on to the next one. Listen for missing sounds. You need to listen to your voice with critical ears, otherwise the careless enunciation will go unnoticed. Would you pass *goverment* for example? How about *intresting, seprit, persnell,* or *confrence*? Don't ignore even tiny words. The word *the* can become a clipped attachment to a word beginning with a vowel, as in *thestimate* or *thoffice.*

Watchoutforatendencytojamwordstogether. Listen for distinct separations between words.

Listen to the pronunciation of the words. Some words are mispronounced by almost everyone; such words include: *schism, junta, irrevocable, clandestine,* and *inexplicable.* Only the most discriminating and critical audience member will be distracted by mispronunciations of these words. But the simple words are another story. Listen for *an* instead of *and, uv* instead of *of, fer* instead of *for,* and *ta* instead of *to.*

The second step in correcting poor articulation is systematically to remove your careless speech habits. Fill in the missing sounds, separate your words, use the correct pronunciations. Listen again and again; keep practicing. In short, work at speaking carefully. Remember, the goal is not flawless articulation and enunciation. The goal is to communicate with an audience without diverting its attention or conveying the wrong impression with careless speech habits.

### If You Have an Accent

Many speakers who have accents or pronounced dialects are unnecessarily concerned about them. In working with hundreds of speakers, I have encountered just one whose accent prevented the audience from understanding parts of the speech. In this case, the speaker was still learning English. Usually it takes two or three minutes for the audience to become accustomed to an accent. After that, they largely ignore it and concentrate on the words.

If you have an accent, remember to speak a bit more slowly in your presentation than you normally do in conversations. It is important that the entire audience understand you. It may take a little time before everyone becomes familiar with your accent, so speak very slowly for the first two minutes or so. Finally, never apologize for an accent or feel self-conscious about it. Most people enjoy the sound of an accent, especially if the speaker pronounces the words carefully.

### Variety

Pace, volume, animation, and pauses are all key elements in effective delivery, but variety is the indispensable ingredient in a listenable voice. Variety means changing the pace to suit the audience's needs: a slower delivery when the material is difficult or when every word must be stressed, faster when the ideas are simple. Variety also means changing the volume, not necessarily from a roar to a whisper— that's a bit too theatrical—but within reasonable limits, for changes in volume add interest and excitement to one's delivery. Notice, incidentally, how experienced speakers often make their most telling points in their quietest voice.

Changes in animation are not only desirable, but in a long presentation they are essential. We are all aware that a monotone eventually causes audience members to drift either into their private worlds or into slumber. The same can be true of a continuously highly animated (or bubbly) voice. The very nature of animation is change—changes in pitch, inflection, and stress. Experienced speakers realize the impact of using short periods of flat, unanimated delivery to set off the highly animated, emphatic peaks in their presentations.

Variety is usually one of the last vocal characteristics we acquire as speakers. It is also the one crucial element in delivery that separates the competent from the accomplished.

## THE BODY

A speaker engages an audience not only with the voice; making contact also requires the use of the entire body. Some parts, however, are more important than others. That makes sense. After all, how much more important is the knee cap as opposed to the eyes?

### The Eyes

The most important features you have for making contact with an audience are your eyes. When you are speaking to an audience, you should be spending *all* of your time looking at their eyes. True, 100 percent eye-contact is impossible. Occasionally it is necessary to glance at notes, or at overhead slides, or at the visual to pick up your next cue, but these brief lapses should account for no more than about 5 percent of the total.

Eye-contact works the same way in presentations as it does in conversations. It tells the listener that you are concerned that he or she is getting the message and reacting to it. Eye-contact tells audience members that you are looking for feedback, that *they* can communicate with *you,* even if their nonverbal message is simply, "I'm listening."

Audience members can easily feel ignored, uninvolved, and neglected when they do not receive eye-contact from a speaker. Likewise, an experienced speaker becomes concerned when someone in the audience constantly avoids contact. Notice the behavior of people in a serious argument. They purposely avoid eye-contact. This is especially true of the person in the listening mode. The tendency is to look away—either downward or often up at the ceiling with an expression of suffering or impatience. The nonverbal message is clear: "You're not reaching me."

Important as it is, eye-contact seems to be ignored by many speakers, especially beginners. They seem fascinated by the floor, or by shoes, wallpaper, or lighting fixtures. Usually their eyes become riveted on the slides or the screen. (Entire presentations have been delivered to a screen!) Sometimes speakers stare pensively off into space, waiting for their next thought to take shape.

Occasionally a speaker with these difficulties claims, "I can't think when I'm looking at someone; it distracts me." Yet the same person has no difficulty whatsoever in maintaining eye-contact during a conversation. We learned to communicate that way as children; it comes naturally to us. Usually what distracts these speakers is the sheer number of people with whom eye-contact must be made. The secret is to apply the easy, natural eye-contact we all use in conversations to larger groups. It's not really difficult. Here are a few tips:

*Look at Everyone*—Some speakers confine their eye-contact to those people in the center, or on one side of the room. It takes extra effort to reach the extreme sides of your audience. By all means make that effort. Never exclude anyone from eye-contact—by the same token, never give any one person excessive amounts of eye-contact. This is especially likely to happen when one person in your audience greatly outranks everyone else. When Mr. Big gets most of the eye-contact it makes him uncomfortable and gives everyone else the impression they are being ignored.

*Do Not Be Trapped*—The screen can have a magnetic attraction for the eyes; so can overhead slides or a demonstration model. Be aware of how much time you are taking away from your audience by staring hypnotically and needlessly at any object.

*Avoid Mechanical Eye-contact*—Eye-contact should be random and natural. Try to avoid looking like a radar dish antenna swinging slowly from left to right.

*Take Your Time*—It takes time to establish contact with audience members. Look at each pair of eyes for at least one full second. Flitting from one face to another is not making contact, but merely going through the motions.

*"Read" Your Audience*—Look for facial expressions, posture, movement, and gestures. Audience members will usually tell you when they agree or disagree, understand or are confused, are keeping up or flagging in their interest. Be ready to react by changing your pace, stopping to ask for questions, or taking a break. Eye-contact benefits the speaker as well as the audience.

### The Hands

Even though we need our hands for an endless variety of useful things (such as dressing, eating, and driving), when most of us get before an audience, our hands become an embarrassment. They loom larger than life. We look for hiding places for them—in our arm pits, behind our backs, in our pockets. Yet the hands can speak an eloquent language of their own if we let them.

The first rule of the hands is that they appear natural. The minimum requirement is that the hands do not become a distraction on which the audience can focus. Playing with pointers, fiddling with chalk or cue cards, scratching repeatedly, fussing with glasses—these and countless similar nervous and pointless uses of the hands only detract from the presentation.

Once we prevent the hands from becoming a distraction, we enter the neutral state where they neither help nor hinder delivery. The hands hang naturally from the sides, or one hand is in a pocket while the other either rests on a table or lectern, holds notes or is simply held in front of the body. In the neutral state, the hands neither add to nor detract from the presentation.

With more accomplished presenters, the hands *add* their own dimension. The hands move to stress or underscore the words, bringing their own expressive dynamics to the delivery. I am speaking, of course, of gestures. I had to sneak up to the word *gestures* because its reputation is a bit tarnished in some quarters. Somehow I can envision a high school teacher admonishing a dull-witted student, "You have to use more *gestures,* Arnold!" No expert in oral communication claims that gestures are mandatory. But neither are spices in food.

The problem with the dictum, "Use gestures" is that many people are uncomfortable moving their hands. The audience shares the discomfort immediately and profoundly. The movements (for the sake of movement) appear wooden, contrived, and inappropriate. It is far better to be yourself—to appear natural—than to make gestures. The curious fact, however, is that nearly *everyone* uses gestures when they speak in everyday conversation. It is natural to do so. (Observe your friends at the next party you attend.) In a presentation, however, the feeling of being on stage inhibits us from letting our hands "speak."

Many speakers deliver their presentations with hands jutting stiffly at their sides, or rubbing together (to generate heat, presumably), or toying with some object. Then after the planned part of the presentation ends, in their response to the questions, the speakers' hands suddenly became natural and expressive. The reason, of course, is that when answering questions we are no longer presenting, but merely responding to one other person, as we would in a conversation.

Here are a few thoughts to help you with your hands, the third most expressive part of your body (after the voice and the eyes):

*Be Natural*—As a minimum goal, your hands should not distract the audience. Do not fiddle with objects or do awkward things with your hands.

*Hold Your Hands in Front of You*—It is best to carry your hands between the waist and shoulders. Try simply placing one hand in the other as you begin. As you warm up, you will begin to use your hands.

*Do Not "Make" Gestures*—Gestures should occur naturally. Never force them; simply allow them to happen. Gestures help you to dissipate nervous energy in a way that enhances communication. They need not be meaningful or pictorial to do so.

*Do Not Use the Same Gesture Repeatedly*—This can be as distracting as the wooden gesture.

*Gestures Should Be Appropriate*—Huge, sweeping gestures are out of place in business presentations; they are much more suited to a football rally. Use gestures to punctuate and stress, to accompany and complement your words.

*Do Not Overdo Gestures*—Occasionally I see a speaker who has a gesture for nearly every word. This is the pinnacle of distraction. Use gestures only for emphasis; otherwise their effect is lost.

*Open the Circle*—Think of your shoulders, arms, and hands as a line. By clasping your hands you form a circle. You also form a circle when you clutch an object, such as a pencil, a pointer, or a lectern with both hands, or put both hands in the pockets. The hands become grounded—incapable of gestures. Try to keep the circle open as much as possible—open to let the audience in.

So much for the hands. What about the rest of the body?

### Posture

We communicate information through the way we hold and use our bodies. Once again, the goal is to be yourself, to be natural.

Figure 16 illustrates the four positions most commonly used by

**A**          **B**          **C**          **D**

**Figure 16** Four Positions to Avoid

untrained speakers, all of which are to be avoided. Positions *A* and *B* are from the military; they are designed to hold the body rigid and motionless. *A* is attention; *B* is parade rest. In time, both seem stiff and unnatural to an audience. Both communicate a sense that the speaker is ill at ease. I call position *C* the police chief posture. It seems to bespeak a kind of threatening authority and, at the same time, a bit of defensiveness. Position *C* solves the problem of what to do with the hands. They are inelegantly stuffed into the arm pits. Position *D* is the most defensive of all. I call it the "genital protective" position, for obvious reasons. Position *D* is to be avoided for two reasons: first, it immobilizes the hands (closing the circle); second, it focusses attention on a part of your anatomy that you prefer your audience would ignore. All of these beginner positions are popular because they solve the problem of what to do with the hands. Each is awkward and tells the audience that you are probably uncomfortable. Other attitudes to avoid include slouching, draping the body over objects, standing with legs crossed, leaning forward severely at the waist, and holding hands on hips.

What is left? Standing reasonably erect, with shoulders back (but not stiffly) and appearing natural and comfortable. That is how you look in a normal conversation. It works beautifully for a presentation, too. Be yourself!

### Movement

When you speak to an audience, motion is inevitable. Even the most rigid stance requires breathing and movements of the jaw and mouth. But how much motion is desirable? Part of what the audience sees is you. You become part of the visual information channel. You, in effect, become part of the message they receive. The simple need for variety and interest require that you change position and even location where possible. The three keys to motion are to *avoid distractions, use motion expressively, and get close to your audience.*

### Distractions

Any constantly repeated movement can become a distraction. Swaying back and forth or from side to side, pacing, rocking, doing a little dance step, or using the same gesture endlessly are all distractions. Other examples of distracting movements include *constantly:*

- removing and replacing or adjusting eyeglasses
- putting hands in and out of pockets

- touching a part of the clothing
- scratching or rubbing the same spot
- playing with objects
- running a hand through one's hair
- readjusting a wayward lock of hair
- sipping water, and/or
- adjusting the microphone

Some movements need not be repeated to be distracting; they are intrusive the first time they are done. Some examples of such motions are: jingling change in the pockets; banging the screen with a pointer; and/or fussing with an overhead transparency—once it is on the projector and reasonably straight, do not try to readjust the visual. The whole screen will be filled with sudden, jerky movements.

Distractions, the enemies of the presentation, come in three varieties:

1. *Preoccupation*—Every audience member has a personal collection of plans and problems that is instantly available to compete with the presentation for attention.

2. *Environmental*—The physical distractions in the room are discussed in Step Six (chapter 7).

3. *Delivery*—The third variety includes not just the distracting movements discussed above, but *anything* the presenter does with the voice or the body to divert the attention of the audience from the content of the presentation.

As the presenter, you cannot change the first variety of distractions; but by eliminating distractions in the environment and in delivery, you *can* hold the attention of an audience and reduce the likelihood that they will slip away mentally.

## Use Motion Expressively

The earlier discussion of gestures may have left you with the impression that they are the exclusive property of the hands and arms. This is not so; we also use the head, shoulders, and torso. President Franklin D. Roosevelt, who was paralyzed below the waist, had a powerful delivery. He used his upper body to heighten and emphasize his points. The magnificent way he tossed his head was a gesture that he could have patented!

When you speak before an audience, your constant companion is nervous energy. The tendency to vent that energy through body motion is hard to repress. The best thing is *not* to repress the energy; use it to move in natural ways that emphasize your ideas. Avoid nervous movement. The most obvious example is perpetual motion. Never move continuously. The vocal principles of the pause apply as well to body motion.

### Get Close to Your Audience

Move as close to your audience as the circumstances will permit. With a little practice, you will develop a sense of just how close you can get to the people in the first row without encroaching on their personal space (about five or six feet). Do not stand in front of one person for long periods. Move naturally to another site in front of your audience.

If your audience is seated in a U-shaped arrangement, do not make the mistake of walking deeply into the U to get close. This forces some audience members to look at an unchanging view of your back (not your best side).

Frequently, you will not have the freedom of movement to get as close to your audience as you wish. If you use an overhead projector, for example, you must remain close enough to change visuals. The worst case, in my opinion, is when you must deliver a presentation while seated. Try to arrange the seats and screen so that you can move about with at least a few feet of leeway.

Lecterns pose several problems. First, they stand between you and your audience. This isolates you and prevents your getting close. Second, the audience can see only your upper torso and head. This view is not very interesting; it is a lot like watching a head-shot on television for an hour. Third, the lectern tends to inhibit *all* movement. Many speakers clutch the top edges of the lectern with a fierce tenacity. Gestures are as rare as items you can buy for a nickel. Fourth, it is too easy for the lectern to become a crutch. You feel comfortable behind there with your notes and your glass of water, and maybe a microphone so you can speak normally. If you grow too accustomed to the lectern, your first presentation without it is likely to be a frightening experience. If you do use a lectern, use it to hold your notes. Be familiar enough with your material so that you can come away from the lectern (at least come out a few feet) and return to it for your next cue. Use it as a reference table, not a crutch.

If you need a microphone, use a lapel or lavalier (neck) mike. Fixed microphones not only immobilize you, but they also cause other problems. If you turn or pull away the sound level falls off. The lapel microphone is always the same distance from your mouth no matter what you do. That means you are free to move about, free to make contact with other than your voice.

## APPEARANCE

Earlier we emphasized that *you* are part of the presentation—part of the visual message. Most of what the audience sees of you is what you are wearing; thus clothing is not a trivial subject. Your appearance is a commentary on the occasion. Your clothing is a nonverbal message on how important you think the presentation is. This notion is not old fashioned, either. People still dress up when they get married or attend functions they deem important. They dress for the occasion. Do not overinterpret this statement. You do not have to don a tuxedo or evening gown to deliver a presentation; but if your appearance is shabby or too casual, you may communicate an unintended message.

It is always a good idea to play down the differences between you and your audience. This applies in a *limited* way to your appearance. When you speak to business groups, wear business clothes. If the occasion is less formal, dress informally but just as carefully.

The wider assortment of clothing that women choose from can pose problems of delivery. If the outfit is especially form-fitting or revealing, a woman speaker can introduce distractions by her mere presence, thus distracting from the message she is there to convey. This does not mean, incidentally, that a woman must dress plainly. It is easy to look feminine and attractive and at the same time professional, for want of a better word. One acquaintance tells me she always takes the most direct approach by wearing an attractive, three-piece business suit. She claims it has the added virtue of boosting her confidence. Men who wear three-piece business suits often share her feelings. But, as mentioned earlier, women do have a much wider range of choices.

One final pointer: occasionally jewelry can be distracting. Audiences tend to notice when jewelry makes sounds or when it is especially striking.

A speaker's appearance is important. Give it some thought.

## NERVOUSNESS

After speaking before audiences for nearly twenty years, I am still nervous when I begin to speak to a new group. In fact, nearly everyone is nervous at first when speaking to an audience, even seasoned performers. The signs are subtle, but if you look for them you can tell when a performer, for example, is working off the itchies and finally arrives at the stabilization point where the nervous energy becomes unobtrusive and productive. You can always expect to be a bit nervous, and this book will not make it go away.

But energy, remember, is vital to effective speaking; good delivery requires heaps of it. The *good* news is that you can harness that primal and destructive nervous energy and use it in productive ways, you can use its power to reach an audience. If you speak to audiences often enough, you will come to realize that you need that energy. Let's look first at the physical side of nervous energy, then examine the frame of mind that causes the problem of nervousness.

### All the Wrong Things

It is curious how unharnessed nervous energy makes us do everything wrong. Breathing is usually the first thing affected. It becomes deeper and more rapid than normal. This causes most people to speak too softly and too quickly, often in bursts. We begin to stumble over our words. In extreme cases, the voice quavers. Our bodies get a bit low on oxygen, causing us to sigh every few minutes. Our saliva and mucus secretions shut down, causing our mouths to get dry, sometimes so dry that the audience can hear the sound of the tongue separating from the palate. The most important tool we have for making contact with an audience—the voice—is usually the first casualty.

But not always: on rare occasions the mind goes blank. It is not that we cannot think; we just cannot think of what we want to say. When this happens to beginners, they usually freeze, which induces a deeper mental paralysis.

The entire body responds to the energy boiling within and seeking escape. The hands clutch at or fuss with objects (pencils, pointers) or with parts of clothing (buttons, rings, neckties). Muscles are so tight they quiver. Some of us pace about ceaselessly if we have room, or do the fox trot if we are short of space. Others stand ramrod straight, every muscle taut as if facing a firing squad. We appear ill at ease, unnatural, uncomfortable—even in pain. These are the normal reactions of a body preparing to deal with danger. Everybody has them and everybody can learn to control them.

### What are You Afraid of?

Let's talk about *fear*. If you wish, use a softer word: why are you (concerned) (apprehensive) (worried) (uneasy)? Take your choice, but nervousness is a primal response to a primal—and normal—emotion: fear.

We react to fear in one of two ways: either by standing our ground and fighting or by running away from the danger. "Fight or flight" is the common expression. (Prizefighters and runners are probably never nervous once their events begin.) How can we respond to the fear induced by the "danger" of a presentation?

We cannot fight anyone; the audience is not the enemy. And even though all our instincts are telling us to flee, we must stand our ground! The result of our inability to respond to the danger shows up in all the destructive ways described earlier. The rapid breathing, the pacing, the restless and aimless movements—all signs of nervousness—are the reactions of a body that wants to run away but cannot. The discomfort and lack of naturalness are saying, "I want to be somewhere else."

What is this danger from which we cannot flee? It turns out to be a many-headed monster. Working with hundreds of speakers has given me the chance to hear why most of us fear speaking to audiences and to get a closer look at the monster's many hideous faces. Here's a partial list:

I have never given a speech before.

I'm no good at speaking to groups.

They may not like me.

I may forget my material.

I may make a fool of myself.

I may fail.

I don't know what may happen.

It will not help much to belittle these real fears, but they are nearly always unfounded. You must look your monster in the eye and ask, "How terrible are you? What is the worst you can do to me? What is the likelihood that you are more myth than monster?"

On a less emotional level, a presentation is a kind of test. Not simply a test of ideas but a test of our ability to present and defend those ideas. As a rule, people do not like tests of any kind. But presentations are tests in which we are exposed; there is no place to hide. When you are standing alone in front of an audience it can be frightening. But there is a special kind of reward in knowing you can pass the test.

### Fighting the Monster

So much for all the negatives; what can be done to control and harness the forces of nervous energy? Plenty; let's begin with the audience. They *want* you to succeed! Bear in mind that *you* are giving the presentation because you know something the audience does not. They are seated out there to receive something from you. The audience expects you to know your subject. They will always give you the benefit of the doubt. In other words, you will have to prove your *lack* of knowledge. Try to remember the worst presentation you ever saw. You probably felt pity for the presenter. What made it a poor presentation was your disappointment in its lack of success. Not only do audiences want you to succeed, but they also expect it.

Now let's focus on you. First, recognize the bind you are in. Your body may respond to the instinct to flee. Decide before you go into the room that you are *not* leaving. You will stand your ground and grapple with the monster. You will use the presentation itself to release the pent-up energy.

Before the presentation, try tensing up your muscle systems— hands, arms, stomach, legs—then slowly relaxing them in turn. This process can help relax your muscles.

Remember that the peak of nervousness always occurs at the beginning of a presentation. Once you get past the first three to five minutes, you will begin to relax and loosen up. Expect to be nervous at the outset. It will pass.

You may choose a light, humorous beginning to help ease you through those first few minutes. This does not necessarily mean telling a joke, but a friendly, humorous interchange between you and the audience can convince you that they probably will not leave their seats and attack you, that giving the presentation probably will not be nearly as painful as you expected.

Use the nervous energy constructively; mobilize it. Move your hands to accent your points. Move your body naturally and get close to your audience. Fill the acoustic space with your voice. Use your eyes and voice to contact everyone in the room. Delivery is *work*. The best thing to do with nervous energy is put it to work.

If you draw a blank mentally, do not *freeze!* Keep talking. It doesn't have to be the specific point you are reaching for, but keep talking about your subject. Look for a handle, something you can grasp to work back into your material. Two things will happen if you keep talking. First, you will find your way back to your outline, and second, the audience will never know you lost your place.

Keep a pitcher of water and a glass nearby to deal with dry mouth. An effective delivery requires normal breathing. If you detect breathing problems, pause. Take a few seconds. Begin to exhale slowly and deliberately. Do not hurry.

One of the best ways to fight nervousness is through preparation. The more thoughtfully and carefully you have prepared, the more confident you will be that you can handle anything that may happen. Careful preparation also allows you to concentrate on your delivery.

Part of effective delivery depends on your feeling good about yourself. Unless you have an unusual problem with self image, you can develop a sense of confidence and well-being by simply practicing and enjoying a few successes.

The best way to combat nervousness is to *practice*. The secret you should know is that destructive nervous energy can be overcome simply by speaking to audiences several times. This kind of practice with your presentation skills is available from an organization called Toastmasters International, a nonprofit, nonpartisan, nonsectarian, educational organization of toastmaster clubs throughout the free world. The address is 2200 N. Grand Ave., Santa Ana, CA 92711. Although I have never joined, the positive experiences of others who have, and a careful look at Toastmaster's literature convince me that much benefit can be derived from membership. Practice can also be had by taking a course in public speaking at your local college or university.

So much for the war of nerves. It is a war we all must fight, but one in which no one need be a casualty.

## WHEN THINGS GO WRONG

It is inevitable; sooner or later something has to go wrong. The visuals will be out of sequence, or upside down. You will say the wrong thing. The projector lamp will blow out. You will lose your place. The screen will roll up with a clatter. You will massacre a word. The possibilities for little flubs to major catastrophes are endless! Here are a few simple tips for dealing with mistakes or unexpected mishaps:

- *Keep going.* Don't panic. Don't stop unless you must. Try not to lose momentum.

- If you have equipment breakdowns, set to work to fix or replace the equipment. You need not suddenly become an entertainer to fill in the time. Simply ask for a few moments time (or, if it's appropriate, take a break).

- Never comment derisively on yourself or your presentation.
- Never apologize for *anything*. It only serves to call attention to, and thus highlight the problem.

## HOW TO USE VISUALS

An important part of a polished delivery is skillfully controlling the visual channel. Using visuals smoothly and unobtrusively is not difficult; like so many other things, it requires an awareness and mastery of an accumulation of small details. This section lists those details.

### In General

Your most urgent concern should be that every audience member can see the visuals. Stand (or sit, if you must) where you will not block anyone's view. Place the screen, easel, or chalkboard where it affords the best view, as discussed in Step Six (chapter 7).

Eliminate distractions. The audience should never be conscious of the equipment or its use. Check out the entire system in advance.

Avoid using notes. Your cues should all be on the visuals. If notes are unavoidable, make them brief and do not fumble with cards or pieces of paper.

Face the audience. Look at the screen or the visual only when it is necessary to pick up your next cue. Visuals have the power to draw the eyes of some speakers and to fix them as if by hypnosis. Use your eyes for making contact with your audience.

Use a long pointer, not your finger. The pointer is designed to focus audience attention on a part of the visual without blocking anyone's view. Do not use it to point at everything; that is distracting. Point out the highlights only. Do not bang the pointer on the screen or chart. Put it down when you do not need it, and (for the last time) do not play with it. Telescoping pointers are especially tempting, by the way; they collapse and expand!

Keep visuals covered until you use them. Cover them up when you are finished with them. Use blank sheets of easel pad paper to cover visuals when you want the audience to focus on the audio channel before or after seeing the visual. With 35-mm, use a slide that fills the screen with a single bright color for the same purpose. White is too glaring. Black is unacceptable because the audience cannot see you. With the overhead projector, simply snap the projector off.

If you must show the same visual twice, make two visuals. Do not waste time fumbling and searching for visuals. Making extra copies of overhead transparencies of 35-mm slides is easy and inexpensive.

Practice using the equipment. Fortunately, most audiovisual equipment is easy to operate. Get familiar and confident with using it. This confidence will allow you to concentrate on your delivery.

In technical presentations, be aware of problems with technical visuals. You may have to explain what a graph or diagram represents before explaining its meaning. Be especially careful about defining conventional technical symbols whenever some audience members may not be familiar with them. (There are still countless people to whom the word *delta* is not the symbol for change, but the name of an airline!)

Here are some tips for handling overhead and 35-mm projection.

### The Overhead Projector

The overhead projector is difficult to use effectively. Most people fail to exploit its advantages. Here are some pointers that can make the difference between ineptitude and professionalism:

- Stand beside the projector. Do not block anyone's view of the screen.

- Never look at the screen. At most, look once after you place each transparency on the projector to be sure all of the image is on the screen. Thereafter, ignore the screen. Glance downward at the visual to pick up your cues. Lower your eyes, not your head. Spend as much time as possible making eye-contact with the audience.

- Once the slide is on the projector, do not touch it until you remove it. Tiny movements of the slide make it look like there's an earthquake on the screen!

- Use a pencil or pen to point out only important features of the visual. Lay the pencil on the visual. If you hold it, the slightest movement will be magnified on the screen. You may also use a grease pencil to underline or circle key points and to write on the visual.

- Use slipsheets between the transparencies, otherwise static electricity can cause them to cling together. Slipsheets make transparencies easier to handle. After you finish with each transparency, remove it from the projector and place it, along with its slipsheet, in a separate pile.

- Try using a copy of the transparency as a slipsheet. You can jot down notes on the slipsheet that will help you cover the key points of a diagram, flow chart, illustration, or other pictorial visual. It is just as easy to glance down at the slipsheet as it is the transparency. Use just a few key topics. Print with large black letters for visibility. You can also use the slipsheet to uncover the visual in stages, when necessary.

- Use transitions between visuals. One minor drawback of the overhead projector is that the transparency must be inelegantly removed from the projector and another visual placed into position for viewing. All of this takes time. Really polished speakers fill that time by linking back to the old slide and introducing the new one.

### Thirty-five mm Projector

Here are several pointers to help you use the 35-mm projector skillfully:

- Stand next to the screen if possible. If you need to use a pointer, get a long one. Hold it in the hand nearest the screen.
- Glance over at the screen to pick up your cues and return immediately to eye-contact with your audience. *Do not deliver your presentation to the screen.* If you point to something, hold the pointer in contact with the screen and look at the audience (not at the spot you are pointing to).
- Some people prefer to use an assistant to advance the slides. To avoid miscues and allow flexibility, operate your own slide control. Of course, the pointer and slide control will keep both hands occupied, but you will be in total control of both channels. Taping the slide control unit to the lectern or table will work well, if you want one free hand.
- Do not totally darken the room. The audience should see you. You are an important part of the visual channel. In a totally dark room, the visuals dominate the presentation. Moreover, your audience cannot take notes. Also, dark rooms induce sleep. Modern presentation rooms have dimmers for the lights.

### Nonprojected Media

The same pointers apply to using flipcharts, easel pads, chalkboards, and other nonprojected media. Avoid distractions, be sure everyone can see the visual, face the audience, maintain eye contact, and use transitions between visuals.

### Preparation

The more carefully you prepare, the more you will be in control of the visual channel. With a little practice, you can master the few techniques that will help you to use visuals with finesse and confidence.

## TONE

Delivery has an important bearing on the overall tone of a presentation. The *tone* is how you come across to an audience. Your tone can be stern, cheerful, serious, friendly, tentative, aggressive, wooden, warm, officious, or aloof. It is composed of the words you choose and the way you say them. Tone is also composed of your facial expressions (or the lack of them), and your posture and body movements. Indeed, virtually every element of delivery we have discussed contributes to the overall tone of your presentation.

In mastering all the elements of delivery, you should strive for a tone that is confident, positive, sincere, friendly, and authoritative: confident without being cocky, positive without being a cheerleader, sincere without being solicitous, friendly without being too chummy, and authoritative without being a know-it-all. When delivering a presentation, be aware that you are communicating on many different levels.

## HANDLING QUESTIONS

We now turn to one of the most vital—and often most overlooked—facets of delivery: the skill of handling verbal exchanges with an audience. It is possible to undermine the gains of an otherwise excellent presentation by an inept handling of the questions and comments of your audience. On the brighter side, when an audience is only marginally in agreement with you, the question and answer session can tip the scales in favor of achieving your objective.

Q. & A. sessions exist for a variety of useful purposes:

- To ensure that the audience understands your subject
- To provide more detail on certain points
- To deal with concerns or doubts on specific arguments
- To provide a forum for airing problems and/or frustrations
- To allow an exchange of views and ideas among audience members

Q. & A. sessions help the presenter gauge the audience's reaction to the presentation—both the level of understanding and the level of acceptance.

Many pitfalls lie in the path of a presenter in these sessions. The next few pages will help you avoid both the major blunders and the minor flaws.

### When Do You Want Questions?

Decide if you wish the audience to ask questions during the presentation, or to hold them until it is completed. Questions asked during the presentation help to clarify confusion or resolve doubts as they arise. In certain kinds of presentations, audience participation is necessary, for example, in a presentation whose objective is to solve a problem. In this case, it is vital that everyone understand the complexities of the problem at every stage of the explanation.

But questions asked during the presentation also can cause problems. As the questions and discussions pile up, your presentation can eventually turn into a meeting. It takes a good deal of skill to keep the engine on the tracks and to avoid spending time on minor points, especially if the audience is composed of high-level executives. It is not unusual, under these conditions, to run out of time before being able to finish. Another problem is that often a question is asked whose answer occurs later in the presentation. The options are to either leave your outline to cover the material out of sequence or to explain, "I'll be covering that point a little later on." Neither choice is especially palatable.

Whether you decide to deal with questions during your presentation or after it, *tell* your audience at the outset; let them know your wishes. One way to postpone questions is to provide everyone with a pad and pencil. Number the visuals. Explain to your audience that you prefer they hold their questions. "Please jot your question down along with the number of the visual. I'll cover all of your questions after I get through the material I have prepared for you."

Whatever your strategy for postponing questions, you must still be prepared for interruptions. This is especially true if the audience is composed of high-ranking executives, who usually tend to speak their piece no matter what ground rules you attempt to establish. Should you be interrupted, simply deal with the question or comment and return immediately to your presentation. Do not give the impression you wish to continue answering questions. Keep in mind, however, that the objective is never to give a presentation. The presentation is a means for achieving an objective. If you are interrupted, by all means be flexible. In some cases, answering questions and *conducting* a discussion will accomplish your objective as readily as will a formal presentation. If you have prepared carefully, your ideas and arguments will prevail in either format.

Your preparation should always include an analysis of the questions you are likely to be asked. Of course, you cannot anticipate every question; but by becoming your own critic, you can predict most of them. The goal is not simply to be ready for questions; it is to prepare the most effective answers.

So much for the preliminaries; here are some guidelines for handling questions.

### Q. & A. Should be a Group Process

Just as a presentation involves every audience member, so should the Q. & A. session. Do not engage in a series of conversations with individuals, but instead be certain that the audience shares both the questions and the answers.

With audiences larger than twenty or so, some people cannot hear every question. Untrained speakers are seldom aware that questions are usually asked in the social communications zone, not the group zone. Develop the skill of judging whether everyone *hears* a question. It is helpful to ask, "Did everyone hear the question?" You will get a better feel for minimum acceptable volume, and your audience members may speak louder. The best solution is simply to repeat the question then answer it. Don't ask the questioner to repeat it, or to speak up.

Having assured that everyone hears the question, next be certain that everyone *understands* it. Audience members possess different levels of understanding. If you are asked a highly technical question, take time to define new terms or to explain unfamiliar material before and during the answer.

Finally, you can maintain a group process by *sharing the answer* with the entire audience. Don't respond only to the questioner; that excludes the rest of your audience. Begin your answer by looking at the questioner, then continue by reaching everyone else with eye contact. Return frequently to the questioner with your eyes, but continue to deliver your answer to everyone.

## Take Your Time

You will often know exactly how you will answer a question long before the questioner has finished asking it. Never communicate that fact. Always hear the entire question, then wait a second or so before answering it. This has two benefits: first, it avoids the embarrassment of cutting off the questioner who may not quite have finished; second, it gives the impression that you are considering the question.

Don't rush your answer. This can create the impression that you want to get the Q. & A. session over, expecially if you seem impatient. Never glance at your watch, for example. Answer the question as completely as necessary. If you suspect that the questioner did not understand the answer, or that the answer did not satisfy the question, test to find out. Either ask, "Does that answer your question?" or simply glance at the questioner and seek nonverbal confirmation. Do not simply rush to the next question.

## Do's and Don'ts for Handling Questions

### Do's

- Do treat every question as legitimate and well-intentioned, even if you suspect it may be designed to trip you up or be destructive.
- Do answer the question directly. Avoid digressions. Get to the point.
- Do be friendly, helpful, and concerned that each questioner is satisfied with your answer.
- If you do not understand the question, say so. You are not expected to be telepathic. Ask for more information or begin your answer by testing your understanding of the question. "Do you mean . . . ?"
- Do answer an inappropriate question directly by explaining that "this question is out of my area of expertise" or "not in the scope of this study," for example.
- Do go back to an appropriate visual if it will help to make your answer clearer or save time.

### Don'ts

- Don't try to bluff your way through an answer. If you do not know the answer, say so. But follow up by asking the questioner to see you after the session is over so that you may arrange to provide the answer. If you are discovered in the act of faking an answer, your credibility quotient drops to zero!

- Don't browbeat a questioner, of course.

- Don't extract humor at the expense of a questioner. No matter how harmless you may think the humor is, someone in the audience may take offense. That someone may not ask an important question because of your earlier humorous thrust.

- Don't indicate that you covered the material earlier. This only serves to embarrass the questioner. Don't even try to do it apologetically: "I guess *when I covered that earlier* I didn't explain it as carefully as I should have." Such attempts only highlight the discomfort.

- Don't answer the question with another question. The Socratic Method is out of place in presentations. You are there to provide answers.

- Don't comment on the question: "Good question!" "I'm glad you asked that question." "Thank you for asking that question." "What a marvelous question!" These cliches waste time. More importantly, if you use them too often, you sound phoney. After a long series of "good question" comments, if you suddenly answer a question without a comment, you imply that the question is without merit.

- Don't use expressions such as "frankly," "to be honest," "to tell the truth," "to be perfectly candid" when answering. These, I realize, are natural responses in conversations, but in the more formal setting of a presentation they may suggest that you haven't been "perfectly candid" until this moment.

- Don't call on somebody unexpectedly. Your audience may contain experts whose assistance with a question may be invaluable. It is all right to ask for help in such circumstances: "There may be someone here who might like to add to my answer." (Pause) But never toss the question to someone: "Charlie has had considerable experience in this area; I'm sure he could explain this much more expertly than I." Poor Charlie. He was sitting comfortably over there in the corner minding his own business. Suddenly he must collect and organize his thoughts to speak to thirty people as an expert. A better, more humane method is to see Charlie *before* the presentation and ask for his help. Be as specific as possible about the information you wish him to provide. Your audience may contain several people whose help you have sought in advance.

## Special Challenges

Q. & A. sessions are enjoyable because they are unpredictable. There is no script, only a plan. And things do not always go according to plan.

You may not get *any* questions. It takes a bit of courage to ask a question in front of an audience. Many people do not enjoy calling attention to themselves. Then there is the risk of asking a dumb question in front of one's peers or superiors. Sometimes the sheer size of an audience inhibits questions.

Here are three ways to help get questions. First, ask in a way that convinces the audience you really want questions, then *wait*. Use a little humor while you are waiting, but give them time to come up with something. Eventually some fearless soul will venture forth. Usually after that first question is answered (skillfully, of course, by you), several hands will shoot up. If waiting does not work, use your own starter questions. Simply explain that several questions are worth exploring. Ask the first one, then answer it. (An alternative is to plant questioners in the audience to ask the starter questions. This method not only seems dishonest, it is unnecessary!) The third method is to hand out cards and ask the audience to write their questions. Questioners can remain anonymous and out of the spotlight. This third technique works especially well with large audiences (more than forty or fifty people).

*E Pluribus, Unum.* This phrase, "Out of many, one," should not prevail during presentations. The Q. & A. period should not be dominated by one person. The audience becomes restless, impatient, irritated. Your job is to maintain control and give everyone air time. Here are a few problem cases:

- *The speechmaker* doesn't really have a question, but wants to comment extensively on everything. It is best to avoid cutting anyone off. Begin by asking the speechmaker, "Do you have a question?" After a reasonable period for the expression of the person's views, you must go on to another question.

- *The zealot* is so interested and enthused about your subject that he or she is not aware that others are being denied time. Try to call on other people. If the problem gets too severe, say something like,

"You seem especially interested in my subject. Rather than take everyone's time here, let's explore it further afterwards."

- *The helper* is never quite satisfied with your answers and is compelled to interpret and amplify each one. It is a way of showing one's brilliance under the guise of being helpful. You may have to tell the helper that the help is not wanted. Much depends, of course, on how much help you are getting.

- *The comedian* likes to use the Q. & A. session to perform. When you get a question whose real purpose is not to get an answer, but to get a laugh, enjoy it. When the same person does it a *second* time, enjoy it a little less (depends on how good the material is). Do not enjoy the third rouser at all, but simply ask for any other questions from the rest of the audience. Remember, you are in charge. The audience expects you to *conduct* the presentation. It is possible to enjoy a sprinkling of humor without having the Q. & A. session develop into a burlesque show.

- *The heckler* disrupts the entire communication process and becomes the focus of attention. Hecklers are so rare in business or technical presentations that it scarcely seems necessary to mention them. If you should ever encounter one, however, remember: You are in charge. The audience is just as irritated with the heckler as you are. They expect you to speak up in their interest.

Remember that whoever asks a question does so as a representative of the entire audience. Treat that person with care. If one person dominates the proceedings, however, that person eventually loses his or her audience membership card. You can see and hear the signs of rejection. The audience begins to tell you, "Take care of this problem so that we can get on with our business."

Another challenge you should be prepared for is ending a Q. & A. session when you do not have time to answer every question. This rarely happens in a business presentation, but occasionally with very large audiences it can pose a problem. One of the best ways to handle it is to explain that not enough time remains to answer every question, that you will answer *three* more. Answer the next question, then announce "Two more." After answering, announce "Last question."

A final word of advice: Q. & A. sessions are full of surprises, unexpected twists, frustrations, and delights. Be ready for anything; and no matter what happens, never lose your composure.

## PUTTING IT TOGETHER

Remember the last time you saw a really effective speaker? Quite likely that speaker was combining all the elements we have discussed and was aiming at one goal: making contact with each member of the audience.

The voice reaching out to the audience was animated and free of noise. The words were said distinctly and you understood them. The pauses and changes of pace, volume, and animation made the voice highly listenable. Not only the voice, but the eyes, face, hands—the entire body and mind—were working to send the vocal and visual messages—the verbal and nonverbal signals—that step-by-step created a sharing of ideas and attitudes.

Good delivery means *engaging* an audience, making contact by using the *energy* within you to reach out and fill the space with your voice and body. Good delivery requires *empathy,* the ability to think and feel as one with your audience, the ability to see and hear the signals they send, and the skill to react to them. Good delivery means establishing a rapport with an audience and creating a climate that encourages questions. It means dealing with questions in a way that involves everyone in the audience. Good delivery does not require mastering a list of actor's tricks. In fact, good actors are experts in convincing us they are someone else. Good delivery is being yourself, allowing your natural style to emerge. In the end, all of these little things add up to the big difference between merely talking to an audience and communicating with one.

# 9
# Some Other Thoughts

Before we part company, here are three or four special ideas on how to improve your presentations.

## A DRY RUN

One important way to improve a presentation is to have a practice run. Usually the stakes must be high enough to justify the expense. Dry runs can be enormously productive if they are conducted properly.

Here are some pointers for getting the most out of a dry run.

- As much as possible, duplicate the conditions of the final presentation, including location, equipment, and visuals.
- Use a live audience—a special audience of critics who are carefully selected to give you feedback.
- Explain to your audience beforehand that you want them to test the presentation for the following ingredients:

    The clarity of the information

    The soundness of the arguments

    The effectiveness of the visuals

    The effectiveness of the delivery

    The overall tone of the presentation
- Also tell them that you want them to ask questions and to evaluate your answers later.
- Time the presentation.

Take notes during the critique, and use the information to perfect the content and polish the rough edges of the delivery of your presentation.

## READING A MANUSCRIPT

Nonprofessionals rarely read manuscripts effectively. Audiences usually find it boring when someone reads to them. Try to avoid reading to audiences at all costs. But if you cannot avoid reading a manuscript, you might as well do it properly. Have the speech typed with very large type and triple space the lines. Have two-inch margins. Do not end lines with hyphenated words. The manuscript should be more than dry words. Go over it carefully and underline the words and phrases you wish to stress. Use parentheses to show where you wish to pause, and arrows to show more or less animation.

The most important element in reading a speech is to make it seem as if you are not reading. It may help to imagine you are speaking normally to one person.

Delivering a speech well from a manuscript requires great skill. You must be so familiar with the speech that you can look away from it frequently and return to it smoothly. Remember: the ideas of the speech are what are important, not the words.

When you glance down at your manuscript, do not lower your head, just your eyes. Spend as much time as possible looking at people, not simply staring into the middle distance.

Whatever you do, strive to sound natural and spontaneous. Some experienced speakers even add an occasional "um" to the delivery to make it sound more human.

## MAKING AN IMPROMPTU SPEECH

An impromptu speech is one in which the speaker is asked to say a few words, either on short notice, or with no notice at all. The impromptu speech is not a frequent occurrence, but should you be called on to deliver one, the following pointers will help you to meet the challenge.

- Don't get caught flat-footed. If you suspect that you may be called to speak, prepare for it from the beginning of the meeting. Take notes on the highlights of the meeting. Jot down the telling points and the people who make them. Use key, trigger words.

- Form your opinions as the meeting progresses. Be prepared to defend them.

- If you are called on, begin with a summary of your impressions. Don't hurry. Use the time to decide on the points you wish to make. Remember, impromptu speeches are informal. The audience is not looking for perfection.

- Use your best delivery tecniques.
- Use the remarks of other speakers as departures for making or emphasizing your points.
- Develop a good closer, or emphatic way of summarizing your remarks.
- If you *are* caught totally by surprise, take time to collect your thoughts. Relate the topic to your past experiences and to your opinions. Above all, be brief. Do not mumble on. Simply make the two or three points worth making and toss it back to the chair.

## USING VIDEOTAPE

Videotaping equipment is probably the best tool available for improving your delivery. It gives you the opportunity to become your own audience. Be prepared for the shock of seeing and hearing yourself for the first time—the camera adds fifteen pounds and ten years. Once you overcome video shock, you can evaluate your voice, posture, movements—your entire delivery technique as an audience member would.

Another advantage of videotape is the ability to replay and study portions of your presentation. The best of all possible worlds is to videotape a dry run then review the tape with the dry-run audience.

## THE VALUE OF PREPARATION

Delivering a presentation is only about 5 percent of the work. Delivery requires speaking words and showing images that were selected, organized, and prepared well in advance of the moment of delivery. Never underestimate the importance of preparation. In fact, if you think about it, this entire book has been designed to help you to prepare for successful presentations.

## LUCK

A conventional way to close is to wish you good luck, but by now we both know that successful presentations are not a matter of luck at all.

My closing wish is that you accomplish your objectives, whatever they may be.